Tracking the White Rabbit

Since its beginning, depth psychology has attempted to change the *status quo* of individual and cultural life by probing beneath surface appearances. This collection of essays looks at aspects of our culture as psychological events instead of framing them as primarily political or even social concerns.

Lyn Cowan explores a number of subjects, considering what possible meanings and implications for change might lie behind the conventional attitudes toward such subjects as:

- Abortion
- Gender and sexuality
- Language
- Memory
- Melancholy

The author puts forward the argument that, although "psychology" and "subversion" are not usually thought of as belonging together, they should be. She argues that a subversive psychology ought not to be confined to the consulting room or limited to clinical diagnoses and treatments. These essays invite the reader to view some of the problematic areas of everyday life from the underside of the psyche. Such a view, presented clearly with humour and insight, offers a way to think differently about usual things, and yields fresh meaning to some of the pressing dilemmas of our time and how we as individuals may respond to them.

Lyn Cowan has worked as a Jungian Analyst since 1980. She served as Director ˙of Training and President of the Inter-Regional Society of Jungian Analysts. She teaches and lectures internationally while making her home in Minnesota.

Tracking the White Rabbit

A subversive view of
modern culture

Lyn Cowan

First published 2002 by Brunner-Routledge
27 Church Road, Hove, East Sussex BN3 2FA

Simultaneously published in the USA and Canada
by Taylor & Francis Inc
29 West 35th Street, New York, NY 10001

Brunner-Routledge is an imprint of the Taylor & Francis Group

© 2002 Lyn Cowan

Typeset in Times by Keystroke,
Jacaranda Lodge, Wolverhampton
Printed and bound in Great Britain by
TJ International Ltd, Padstow, Cornwall
Cover illustration by Martha Osterberg
Cover design by Louise Page

British Library Cataloguing in Publication Data
A catalogue record for this book is available from the British Library

Library of Congress Cataloging-in-Publication Data
Cowan, Lyn, 1942–
    Tracking the white rabbit : a subversive view of modern culture / Lyn Cowan.
        p. cm.
    Includes bibliographical references and index.
    ISBN 1–58391–198–7 (pbk.)
    1. Psychoanalysis and culture. 2. Jungian psychology. 3. Jung, C. G.
    (Carl Gustav), 1875–1961. I. Title.
BF175.4.C84 C69 2002
150.19′54—dc21   2001043344

ISBN 1–58391–198–7

For Bonnie,
who fortunately never finds my excuses credible

Contents

. . . when the Rabbit actually *took a watch out of its waistcoat-pocket*, and looked at it, and then hurried on, Alice started to her feet, for it flashed across her mind that she had never before seen a rabbit with either a waistcoat-pocket, or a watch to take out of it, and burning with curiosity, she ran across the field after it, and was just in time to see it pop down a large rabbit-hole under the hedge.

In another moment, down went Alice after it, never once considering how in the world she was to get out again.

(Lewis Carroll, *Alice's Adventures in Wonderland*)

Acknowledgments

No book is written in a vacuum, and writing is not a solo act. Many fingerprints besides mine are on this book, invisible but there, in the contributions of the many people who helped me in many ways time and again. Thoughtful students, energetic workshop participants, astute audience members, encouraging colleagues and constructive critics, have all helped formulate and refine ideas and have pointed me in new directions just when tracking the White Rabbit seemed to leave me in a cul-de-sac.

Most especially I am thankful to my friend and editor, Bonnie Fisher, to whom this book is dedicated. It was she who suggested, pressed, badgered, cajoled, and finally pulled it into the light of day. Those who read the final draft deserve more thanks than I can write here: Pat Berry, Jan Bauer, Claudette Kulkarni, Andrea Steffens. They responded enthusiastically and with honesty and patience as I wavered and backtracked and lurched ahead. Thanks also to Andrew Samuels, who opened a door, and to the editors at Routledge, Kate Hawes who was my first contact and advocate, and Dominic Hammond, who patiently guided me through the intricacies of readying the book for print. Kristin Susser proved a most capable production editor, and Kate Trench, who has a sharp eye for details in context, is a first-rate rabbit tracker.

Finally, I want to thank a young man named Carl, who in his secret, real life is a poet, but who works as a computer technician at Best Buy and spent many patient hours – for which he (subversively) did not charge me – rescuing the manuscript in its entirety when my computer crashed. I neither could have nor would have rewritten the more than 75 percent of the text trapped in the dying hard drive, so the whole thing would have died with it. On such seemingly small encounters and unexpected occurrences do the best laid plans and dreams of authors depend. And such unplanned happenings, too, are one of the ways in which you might catch a glimpse of and begin tracking the White Rabbit.

Further acknowledgments:

"The Autumn Sonnets." Copyright © 1972 by May Sarton, from *Collected Poems 1930–1993* by May Sarton. Used by permission of W. W. Norton & Company, Inc.

Quotation from *Re-Visioning Psychology* by James Hillman, copyright © 1975 by James Hillman, used by permission of HarperCollins Publishers, Inc.

Quotation from *Myths and Mysteries of Same-Sex Love and The Goddess*, copyright © 1989 and 1984 respectively, by Christine Downing, Crossroad Publishing Company. Used by permission of the author.

Excerpt from Ovid, *Metamorphoses*, translated by Rolfe Humphries, copyright © 1955 by the University of Indiana Press, Bloomington, Indiana and Indianapolis. Used by permission of the publisher.

Quotation from Audre Lorde, "Zami: A New Spelling of My Name," in *Deep Down: The New Sensual Writing by Women*, ed. Copyright © 1988 Farrar, Straus & Giroux. Used by permission of the publisher.

Quotation from Murray Stein, "Narcissus," in *Spring: Archetypal Psychology and Jungian Thought*, copyright © 1976 by The Analytical Psychology Club of New York. Used by permission of the author.

Lines from Hesiod's *Theogony*, translated and copyright by Dorothea Wender, Penguin Classics, 1973. Used by permission of Penguin Books Ltd.

Preface

This collection of essays spans nearly twenty years, but it was only while rewriting and assembling them for this book that the theme of subversion emerged as clearly as it did. So the first essay is also the introduction, not so much to ensure thematic coherence of all the essays, but to articulate an attitude inherent in each of them. It has grown out of early lectures on the subject of what I might call "normal deviance" and particularly a lecture given originally in 1987, subtitled "Jungian Psychology as Subversion." It never crossed my mind, at that time, that the lecture was a seed – or thorn – that had begun and would continue sprouting in all my earlier and subsequent work.

Of course, many others in the field have simultaneously been writing and working on similar themes, but just as each of those works is distinctive in some way, so is this one. Many of these essays could not have incorporated new and then-future work of other authors, so I ask the reader's forbearance at the absence of recognition or acknowledgment of those who appeared in print before me. Such absence is only a result of timing and circumstance.

I first began tracking the White Rabbit in 1982 in an essay entitled, "Tracking the White Rabbit: Notes on Eccentricity," presented to an audience in Denver, Colorado. The lecture originally focused on the idea of eccentricity as important to understanding individual character, as well as gently critiquing Jung's model of the psyche with a single center (the Self). Since the appearance of James Hillman's two excellent books which have the idea of "character" as their central theme (*The Soul's Code*[1] and *The Force of Character*[2]), I reworked much of my own essay to move it in a different direction. The idea of Wonderland as a complementary reality, not a contradictory one, was developed in an address given to the psychiatric and psychology staff of Golden Valley Hospital in Minnesota. The paper was met with stony-faced silence by the extremely traditional and medical-minded staff, which unnerved me a little, but I confess to being inordinately gratified the following day when a colleague called to tell me that the Chief of Psychiatry had warned his staff members to "pay no attention" to anything I had said and that I was "a dangerous woman." What higher compliment? I decided then and there that tracking the White Rabbit was my true calling and I would not abandon the pursuit.

"Feeding the Psyche: Junk Words and Corn-Fed Music" reflects my concern with language and the way psychology uses or abuses it. This has been a fundamental theme for me since my training days in Zurich in the mid-1970s, when I began to realize that the jargon of psychology was not used only by analysts but by psychologists of all varieties, and that the implication of "empty words" was a far-reaching cultural problem. The essay went through several formulations from its first presentation in 1989 at a conference on Women and Spirituality in Minneapolis, but this version is the most complete.

The essay on "Women and the Land: Imagination and Reality" is a bit of a departure from the others in that it is the most personal (but not private) and its style is deliberately that of a reminiscence. Its audience was a large group of women from practically all ethnic and religious backgrounds at a conference in 1988 on land and women's approaches to conserving and managing it. Since most of the participants were rural women, many of them operating stock and crop farms, I felt rather an outsider and wondered why "on earth" I had been invited to say anything at all. But I was grateful for the opportunity to even think about a subject "foreign" to me, and especially for the warm reception given to me and my words.

The essay on the always-hot topic of abortion, "Taking the Dark With Open Eyes," is an expanded version of a paper presented at the University of Minnesota at a program on that subject sponsored by the Minnesota Jung Association in 1992. This was one of my first efforts to apply a psychological attitude, and particularly an archetypal approach, to a besetting cultural problem which has always been framed in other terms. Along with the 1994 essay, "False Memories, True Memory, and Maybes," it was later published in an anthology of essays on contemporary cultural themes (*The Soul of Popular Culture: Looking at Contemporary Heroes, Myths and Monsters*[3]), and I am taking this opportunity to thank the editor of that volume, Mary Lynn Kittelson, for asking me to contribute to it.

"Styx and Stones: Hatred and the Art of Cursing" is an essay that, like the others in this book, reflect my interest in topics which usually fall into a shadow realm of experiences and emotions that are important but definitely unattractive, unappealing, and seemingly unconstructive. In

1985 an academic colleague at Augsburg College in Minneapolis invited me to give a lecture as part of the college's annual Faculty Series lectures. I cannot now imagine what in the world possessed me to write a paper on hatred and cursing, a subject sure to call forth the same emotion it was addressing. I must have been either very brave, very foolish, or very angry, but the latter two are the most likely. It was a great relief when no one threw eggs or stones at me, and in fact, the lecture was very well received – whereupon I foolishly went and gave it again in two other cities. Then, deciding not to press my luck, I put it away in a drawer, where it has sat for the last fifteen years, until now.

Just before I moved into a new home in late 1990, my friend Christine Downing called and asked if I would write an essay on the "Archetype of the Victim" for an anthology she was editing, called *Mirrors of the Self*. My initial response was to decline, on grounds that (1) the company with whom I would appear in print was too august (Jung, von Franz, Downing, Hillman, Berry, many esteemed others), and (2) I would be living out of boxes while major remodeling was being done and I wouldn't have either desk or access to books and probably wouldn't be able to find a pencil, let alone get my computer set up. Couldn't make the deadline, I insisted. Chris insisted more strongly and won out. The essay turned out to be, I thought, a disaster, but it was the housing circumstances that made me blind to anything good – an over-budget project that took three weeks longer to finish than expected, in the dead of winter with no heat. (Not optimal conditions in Minnesota.) During the days the workmen climbed over me to get to the bathroom as I sat hudded over unopened boxes with my computer monitor and keyboard perched precariously on top. Christmas came and went. I muttered my way through the writing, reminding myself I was lucky to have a roof over my head at all but feeling victimized anyway. Fortunately, Chris was pleased with the result, the addition was completed, the heat came back on, and my mood lightened considerably.

The first thing I did once I had my study habitable was begin writing "Homo/Aesthetics, or, Romancing the Self," again in response to an invitation to contribute to an anthology. That volume, *Same-Sex Love and the Path to Wholeness*[4] (edited by Robert Hopcke, Karin Lofthus Carrington and Scott Wirth), was the first collection of essays on the subject of homosexuality by Jungian analysts and Jungian-oriented psychotherapists. Though the time between the "Victim" essay and "Romancing the Self" was quite brief, the tonal difference is pronounced, not only because of the stark difference in subject, but because I was a lot warmer and comfortable when I wrote it.

The essay called "Sexual Encounters of the Third Kind" emerged as a much shorter, distilled lecture from what had become a monograph ("Dismantling the Animus") on the subject of Jung's animus theory. In the time between the writing of the animus essay (1993) and this book, several Jungian authors have taken up the debate and made great contributions to rethinking problems in Jung's theory. "Dismantling the Animus" appeared recently on the web at the C. G. Jung Page (www.cgjungpage.org), but the ideas in it were presented first as lectures in several cities, specifically on the animus, and then evolved into a lecture with a different emphasis: sexuality rather than the animus. Trying not to be too academic about an academic subject which, when lived, should never be academic, was a bit of a trick. I tried to have a little fun with the subject, and to give it the attention which, it seemed to me, Jungians tend to avoid giving it, and about which all of us may assume too much and know too little.

The last essay in this collection, "Blue Notes: Some Reflections on Melancholy," is actually the oldest in terms of my interest, and also the first of what I hope comes after this book. I have been working sporadically on a book on melancholy for years – one of those projects that seem to take a lifetime, and this one probably will – with the essay in this present form a small paring of the larger work still in progress. Presented first at the Medical College of Virginia and later in Pittsburgh, both in 1994, the rather skeletal main ideas in the essay have been taking on flesh and growing into a full-length manuscript. And so it seemed fitting to end the book with an essay that is a bridge to the beginning of something else, or, more likely, one that means tracking the White Rabbit down another hole.

Notes

1   James Hillman, *The Soul's Code: In Search of Character and Calling*, New York: Random House, 1996.
2   James Hillman, *The Force of Character and the Lasting Life*, New York: Random House, 1999.
3   Mary Lynn Kittleson (ed.), *The Soul of Popular Culture: Looking at Contemporary Heroes, Myths and Monsters*, Chicago: Open Court Publishing Co., 1998.
4   Robert H. Hopcke, Karin Lofthus Carrington and Scott Wirth (eds), *Same-Sex Love and the Path to Wholeness*, Boston: Shambhala, 1993.

Introduction

Soul is the living thing in man, that which lives of itself and causes life. . . . With her cunning play of illusions the soul lures into life the inertness of matter that does not want to live. She makes us believe incredible things, that life may be lived. She is full of snares and traps, in order that man should fall, should reach the earth, entangle himself there, and stay caught, so that life should be lived. . . .[1]

(C.G. Jung, Archetypes of the Collective Unconscious)

Nothing is ever the same as they said it was. It's what I've never seen before that I recognize.[2]

(Diane Arbus)

As a child, I never trusted anything I could see easily and never fully believed anything I was told if it sounded too assured. This unwilling skepticism did not give me a lot of security. But it did nurture a tendency to subversion which I only now, well into middle age, can recognize as the way I've always gotten through life, and still do.

I'm fairly certain I am one of many who are born with a subversive gene. In my case, it must have been lurking at the bottom of the pool, a throwback inclination to ancestors forgotten by the rest of my relatively conventional family. I imagine those ancestors expressed the genetic influence to subversion through rebellion against the Czar, underground guerilla activities in various wars, illegal sexual orientations, and writing inflammatory headlines for labor union newsletters. Next to these brave ancestors, my own subversive activities pale in significance. Only twice in my youth I tried – and then timidly – to change the *status quo*: once, in 1959, when I refused to sign the loyalty oath required of New York State high school students in order to graduate, which required me to swear that I was not then nor ever had been a member of the Communist

Party nor had sought to subvert or overthrow the government of the United States so help me God; and second, when I stopped on a street corner in Manhattan that same year and signed a petition for some cause that seemed worthy, which also gave me a subscription to the Communist or Socialist Party's (I wasn't sure which) *Daily Worker*. I never received an issue of the newspaper or heard from any member of the party, but I worried for years that the FBI would track me down, throw me in front of the merciless House Un-American Activities Committee, and I would die in prison, too young. I expected to live a short, tragic life, which encouraged my adolescent romantic melancholy.

It took me until I was past forty to discover that I would take a psychological path to express the subversive gene I carried. I found that I was a much better subversive by becoming as much a realist as a romantic, and by doing psychological analysis with real people with as much clarity of vision as possible.

The subversive gene does not confer the courage of conviction. In fact, it has nothing to do with convictions, or courage. The genetic inheritance to subversion merely gives you a compulsion to look through ideas and experiences to the underside, making you something of a psychological snoop. It makes for intolerance of the *status quo*, whatever the *quo* is, and thus compels a different vision, a skewed vision, of what appears to be conventional, obvious, usual. Something in the psyche – which I am metaphorically calling the "subversive gene" – wants to subvert whatever is there, turn it under and upside down, examine it from the bottom, find some odd detail that will capsize the accepted view. Issues of political debate, theological doctrines, psychological theories, social norms, everyday speech, usual ideas of sex and emotion – all are grist to the subversive mill, for they make up the cultural assumptions by which we live but which we do not see clearly. Still a romantic at heart, I want nothing less than to change the culture, to make it a psychological, soul-serving culture. But changing the culture can be done in small ways, just as small snapshots may be just as compelling and significant as billboard-size blow-ups.

If a subversive attitude is not inherited, it can be learned. You can learn to cultivate a subversive vision, by which I mean cultivating a psychological perception, seeing down and into and through to whatever is lying just out of sight, in the dark. Though it happened inadvertently, it was a happy mating for me when my subversive tendency joined my love of photography, and helped temper my romanticism with black-and-white reality. A subversive vision takes seriously the old saying that there is more than meets the eye, and a subversive attitude will then try to change, or at least think differently about, whatever the eye meets.

But once subversion as a psychological approach to life is taken seriously, one sets out on a course that winds ever downward, attempting ever more penetrating insight. It leads to a deepening sense of restlessness – even distrust – that disturbs every cliché, every assumption, every cherished value, subverts it and turns it under, over, around, until some new idea breaks through, some fresh meaning is revealed. Or, if nothing quite this grand, then at least until there is a quiet gasp of delight at having found a little piece of mystery in the mundane.

Jungian psychology has been most compatible to my subversive turn of mind. It is less a set of doctrines than an attitude toward experience, less a system of thought than a way of perceiving what *is* thought, less a technique of clinical practice than a perspective on the human psyche, including its ailments. I am always a little surprised that among the many epithets given to Jungian analysts, "subversive" is not usually one of them.

There are people who disregard Jungian psychology and the practice of analysis because they think of it as unscientific, or occult, or theoretically dense, or as having no practical application. But the real reason for their disregard or hostility is that a psychology of depth poses a vital threat to the *status quo*, for it takes all the traditional values, takes the conventional perception of the world and one's place in it, and subverts it, turns it under so that the hidden parts of life, the roots and source, may be examined in privacy, slowly and with care.

I am interested in the aspects of Jungian psychology that really are threatening in some way. In other words, behind the almost placid persona of Jungian psychology is a shadow, a dimension of thought and psychotherapeutic practice that poses a potential threat to established values and assumptions, and that works toward a chronic discontent with the *status quo*. Jungian psychology is a sub/versive psychology. It not only turns things under to get at the roots of individual psychopathologies (and finds quite a different understanding of them), it is subversive in the political sense as well, attempting to change the culture by altering individual perceptions of and participation in it.

The idea of "change" is popular in modern psychology, but it, too, has a shadow: the most heroic of American values has been the notion that anything or anyone can, with sufficient exercise of willpower and a little help from friends, change anything one wants, and the moral imperative is that such change must always be for the better. This view of change inflates it and makes it moralistic and unrealistic, placing a heavy burden on individuals who *cannot* change and who are not moral wretches because of that. Not everything in the individual psyche can be, or should be, changed, any more than a cottonwood tree should be required to change its appearance to that of a redwood because redwoods are bigger, more impressive, and privileged to live in federally protected national parks.

But of course there are kinds of change that are possible, desirable, and necessary. Maintaining the *status quo* is harmful and destructive to living organisms. Yet even though change is the first principle of life, it is also deeply threatening to human beings, who, of all species, ought to know better. The field of psychology generally has not been the proving ground for change. Too often the profession has allied itself with the political establishment, aligned itself with the economic power base, and sought the prestige of scientific medicine. It has not seen itself in the vanguard of cultural renaissance, but contents itself – perhaps sullenly – with its position as the bastard child of medicine, voluntarily wearing the clothes of the medical model while complaining about the poor fit. Psychology looks to science as the validating metaphor rather than art, as if these must be mutually exclusive.

In its vocabulary and the way it uses language, psychotherapy lends unconscious support to our culture's preoccupation with upward growth, forward progress, and a morality based on law instead of Eros.[3] Words and phrases become personas, static masks, while the shadow behind them hides their subjective, substantial meanings, with harmful consequences. Popular psychology's jargon needs subverting because it has become our common vocabulary which actually prevents us from saying, or even knowing, what we really mean. Words such as *issues, safety, appropriate, commitment, wellness*, are just a few modern buzzwords that reduce our subversive capacity and delude us into assuming that these dead concepts are living experiences. As we learn to think and talk about ourselves in this vocabulary of generalizations, we seem to be increasingly unable to differentiate emotions from their consequences, and concepts from experiences.

I worry that a flattening of psychic life is setting in, that the West as a collective being is showing all sorts of psychopathic tendencies. This need not be validated by a rise in violent crime and homicide rates, or the number of serial killers on the loose. It is validated by the escalating need for external stimulation through entertainment, in the fear and distrust of the intensity of deep emotion (any emotion), in the absence of genuinely new and interesting ideas in public discourse, and in the boredom of psychotherapy and its insipid egocentric theories. While psychology as a profession is not entirely to blame for this unhappy intellectual and emotional flattening, it has been too much an accomplice.

I have a near-mystical belief in the idea that any deep, thorough-going change of attitude and perspective in an individual life changes the collective mind and shifts the collective psyche, if only by a millimeter, in the same way that a good photograph changes our perception of its subject in the most subtle, subliminal way. Every time a single person challenges an assumption, breaks a habit, alters an old family pattern, understands a dream, is struck with a realization, turns memory into art, acts on a tiny, tenuous insight – every time, the collective psyche shifts and the entire species is affected we are all a little changed by it.

Quality subversion takes time. It isn't just what depth psychologists do that bothers some, it's that they take so long doing it. There must be something subversive in a course of therapy, like depth analysis, that takes more time than six weeks and more money than insurance will cover. It moves at its own pace according to individual rhythm quite apart from the collective imperatives of speed, cost efficient methods, "objectively measurable" results. Impatience is the shadow of short-term therapy and that shadow is projected on to long-term analysis, where it is perceived as narcissistic indulgence or ineffective technique.

The subversive process of examination of and from the underside is also what alchemy called a process of "corruption" of the material in the vessel, and much of Jungian analysis works through corruption. If successful, it also works through corrosion. The analytic approach is not only supportive and nurturing and insightful, it is also cutting and separating and has an acidic quality, cutting through naïvety and ways of seeing that are useless or personally destructive. It eats away at the unquestioned rightness of values we have inherited, ideas we have assumed, images that unconsciously govern and compel us.

The idea of subversion, with its political overtones and associations of instability and revolution, has itself been cast into the shadow. Anyone undertaking to work in shadowy areas – including those involved in depth psychology – takes on some of the characteristics of the subversive: a growing discontent, if not outrage, against collective systems which are damaging to individual life; a deepening resistance to majority thinking (*even when one agrees with it*); new survival skills within one's profession so as not to be eaten by corporate greed and disloyalty; and the ability to live one's real life "underground," keeping the new changes of great value hidden from profane and persecuting eyes. One begins almost to lead a double life, one above ground going about in the world, giving out business cards, collecting fees, making a living, making love, all that – and another life, deeply subverted underground. Both lives are eminently real, each of critical importance: not paranoid dualism, but a doubleness.

Similar to a "double exposure" in photography, "doubleness" here means neither duplicity nor oppositional dualisms. It means having a sort of double vision which is not astigmatism, but clear-sightedness of two or more visions: one eye looks through the camera lens, while the other eye remains open and takes in whatever is not in the viewfinder.

Jung observed that the unconscious psyche is, paradoxically, both conservative and creative. On the one hand, he says, the collective psychic heritage of our species is made up of the "accretions of millenia – instincts, functions, archaic forms and reactions." It is also an "intricate web of archetypal conditions," modes of perception of characteristic situations that tend to evoke the same possibilities of response, over and over again. "Thus," says Jung, "the unconscious is seen as the collective predisposition to extreme conservatism, a guarantee, almost, that nothing new will ever happen."[4]

Then Jung went right on to say,

> If this statement were unreservedly true, there would be none of that creative fantasy which is responsible for radical change and innovations . . . Generally speaking, [such a change or innovation] is an intrusion from the realm of the unconscious, a sort of lucky hunch, different in kind from the slow reasoning of the conscious mind. Thus the unconscious is seen as a creative factor, even as a bold innovator, and yet it is at the same time the stronghold of ancestral conservatism. A paradox, I admit, but it cannot be helped.[5]

And perhaps it is just as well that it cannot be helped. An attitude that requires only a single explanation, a perspective that sees problems only in terms of solutions instead of interesting complexities, is an attitude that cannot tolerate paradox. It is an attitude Jung described as "neurotic" because it is one-sided and requires that all complexities and difficulties of life be reduced to single answers, solutions, or clichés. (Or that can be arranged in Seven, Ten, or Twelve Steps and sold in paperbacks everywhere.) The attitude that cannot tolerate paradox is psychologically immature, unable to withstand and endure complicated human emotions and motivations, impatient with reflection and serious thought, and harshly judgmental about all those creative intrusions coming from deeper sources. It is, unfortunately, an attitude that characterizes much of Western political life these days and has always marked the shadow side of the scientistic attitude. But if it is true that psyche is by nature paradoxical, then where we cannot hold paradox we lose psyche.

Jung saw analysis as something of a paradox too: the doctor attempting to help the patient to a normal and reasonable life, working towards an adaptation to reduce suffering and increase a sense of well-being. But the definitions of "normal" and "reasonable" are social constructs, not *a priori* categories. And so Jung advises, more than once, that we "follow nature as a guide," and he says, "what the doctor then does is less a question of treatment than of developing the creative possibilities latent in the patient himself."[6]

Now, anytime you encourage creative possibilities in an individual you are encouraging subversion, because creative possibilities are rarely used to maintain the *status quo*, either in individual or collective life. Most people come into therapy because they are uncomfortable, unhappy, or downright miserable with the way things are: themselves, their lives, their jobs, the families that spawned them, the systems which govern them. They come with all manner and degrees of depressions, repressions, and intolerable oppressions. If we deal only with the personal dimension of their disturbance, the collective *status quo* is undisturbed, and this is another form of repression. The truly subversive activity is to locate, identify and expose the collective systemic problem at the root of the personal problem, so it can be seen how such systems limit or destroy individuality. The roots of all the *isms* – capitalism, funda-mentalism, feminism, sexism, racism, heterosexism, anti-Semitism, communism – need to be examined for the patterns and depressions they make in a person's life. Once the basic assumptions by which a person lives begin to be subverted, creative possibilities appear in the wings, off-stage in shadow, ready to make an entrance when the play calls for another "role."

It is the psyche's creativity that does the subverting in the end, not the analyst or Jungian theory. I don't consider casting around for new cognitive schemas or conscious behavior-changing techniques "creative," although they are useful for specific purposes. I am referring rather to the wild creativity of spontaneous imagination, of fresh images, invading in bizarre, outrageous, amazing, sometimes shocking ways, but which bring dramatic new themes and scenarios for your life, your past, your future, your abilities, your capacity to love – possibilities of profoundly changing your sense of yourself. Subversive possibilities.

Everything we have learned in this lifetime and the ideas we have received from preceding generations must be articulated and challenged – not because they are wrong and must be corrected, but because they cannot be truly our own until we do. Each individual must decide their worth for her or himself – whether to discard or preserve, whether to keep intact or alter slightly. This is an analysis of shadow-stuff, a constant application of a corrosive attitude that tests what is necessary and valuable and dissolves that which is useless and harmful.

In clinical practice, a "successful" analysis is a corrosive process, eating away like acid at the dearest values, the most obvious assumptions, the most cherished images of who we are, corrupting our sense of the world as a place where we might expect justice if we are innocent (for we are not innocent), truth if we do not consciously lie (for we often lie unconsciously), honor if we do not betray family traditions (but we must betray them if we are to grow up), and acceptance if we conform to the bedrock values that have been ingrained in us (but the price of acceptance is too high, we cannot conform or we die of suffocation).

The end of such an analysis might produce a successful misfit: a person who holds the paradox of profound identification with the rest of humanity, but whose individual identity sets him or her at the periphery of the human community. Such a person lives in close community with a sense of being peripheral at the same time. Not marginal, but peripheral. This person's life has been subverted, turned under, made double, expanded to hold paradox and see creative possibilities as welcome intrusions. This person perceives much of life from the underside, the shadow side, and by simply living this sense of the peripheral life, may influence the mass of the center to change. Such persons embody the shadow of the society in which they live, and are perceived to be threatening, dangerous, crazy, subversive, deviant, even criminal – even if they keep their lawns mowed and pay their bills and wear seat belts when driving.

One last word about the making of a subversive, even a shy and reluctant one. My father was an artist who drew comic books for a living. In America in the 1950s this was considered a subversive activity. Americans were choked with fear about Communist plots to overthrow the United States government by subverting American youth. (Never mind that my father's work was drawing red-blooded heroes like cowboys and Captain America.) The powerful House Un-American Activities Committee decided at the time that comic books caused juvenile delinquency and made the youth of America vulnerable to Communist propaganda. Reading comic books, said the old congressmen, destroyed moral fiber and the innocence of youth and turned children instantly into violent, godless revolutionaries.

Of course, like millions of other kids, I read comic books as part of my literary diet, and I can tell you, more than forty-five years later, that Congress completely misread the source of my corruption. Comic books had nothing to do with the fact that, by the age of eleven, I was already having creative fantasies about overthrowing everything that was making me crazy: dress codes at school, anti-Semitism, rules for being a girl that warped my self-image, the whole oppressing gray flannel conformity by which we all had to live. The very values Congress was trying to preserve drove me psychologically underground, from where I began to emerge some years later in Jungian analysis, far more subverted by that process than by any comic book I ever read.

Or, maybe it was the gene.

Notes

1. C.G. Jung, "Archetypes of the Collective Unconscious," in *Collected Works*, vol. 9, i, Princeton: Princeton University Press, 1959, para. 56.
2. Doon Arbus and Marvin Israel (eds) *Diane Arbus*, New York: Aperture Monographs, 1972, flyleaf.
3. In Greek mythology, Eros was called "the first-born and fairest of the gods," who personified desire and the force that brought things together in relationship. In later myths, he was thought to be the son of Aphrodite, thus uniting people in love. With these characteristics, Jung considered Eros the "principle of relationship," the psychological capacity to form relationships based on love and desire, and he posited this principle in contrast to the psychological principle of Logos, which is concerned with intellectual reasoning and logical analysis. I use the term "Eros" here with much the same meaning Jung gave it, but it is capitalized in order to keep the divine "person" alive in the "principle."
4. C.G. Jung, "Some Aspects of Psychotherapy," 1929, in *Collected Works*, vol. 16, Princeton: Princeton University Press, 1966, para. 61.
5. Ibid., para. 62.
6. C.G. Jung, "The Aims of Psychotherapy," 1929, in *Collected Works*, vol. 16, Princeton: Princeton University Press, 1966, para. 82.

Chapter I

Tracking the White Rabbit

Notes on eccentricity

(or, A quick tour with Alice through Wonderland)

> "The time has come," the Walrus said,
>   to talk of many things:
> Of shoes – and ships – and sealing
>   wax – of cabbages and kings –
> And why the sea is boiling hot –
>   and whether pigs have wings."
>   (Lewis Carroll, *The Walrus*
>   *and the Carpenter*)

My first note on eccentricity must be a disclaimer: I am completely incompetent on the subject of ships and sealing wax, have never met a king, and dislike cabbage. I will get to pigs and the boiling sea later. For now, I can say something about shoes, those metaphorical soles that give us a "standpoint," the habitual attitude on which we stand our ground and regard the world, and in which someone else must walk a mile if they are to understand our experience.

Eccentricity is important because it is one of the ways an individual is quietly subversive, undermining whatever is conventional, unquestioned, passively assumed. It is the quintessential expression of personal style, since eccentricity is not so much *what* one does as the *way* one does it. Being slightly off center or out of center (*ex centric*) also challenges our comfortable ideas about sanity and rationality and the value of logical thinking.

Of course, the English first spring to mind when it comes to eccentricity. They have a corner on it. As the French are famous for love and the Italians for opera and the Russians for vodka, the English have always been a nation of eccentrics. The reason for this is given by the poet and critic Dame Edith Sitwell, herself an example and author of a book on the subject: eccentricity is a particularly English characteristic, she says, "because of that peculiar and satisfactory knowledge of infallibility that is the hallmark and birthright of the British nation."[1] Eccentricity is the art of being infallibly right about the most ordinary things: how to dress, dinner table manners, patterns of thought, appropriate behavior. Each eccentric personality has an odd twist on these categories, which make their expression a matter of personal style rather than an overt clash with collective rules.

It would seem, then, that knowing your infallibility – where you are right – is a prerequisite for being a real eccentric. And though this knowledge may be a matter of passionate, even obstinate, conviction, it is not the same as being self-righteous. Eccentricity is not about other people; it does not make comparisons, it is not relational. Dame Sitwell's notion of eccentricity recognizes that one's "infallibility" is really an amplified explanation of oneself – a showing forth of your essential character – and firmly refusing to be anything other than what you are.

Eccentrics are stubborn; they cannot be dissuaded because they know they are infallibly right. They know which end of the boiled egg to crack. They know without reading a newspaper or watching CNN which candidate *should* be elected. They can tell infallibly the difference between true gossip and false rumor. They are infallible authorities on matters of family and morals, and they are experts at knowing which closets hold family skeletons, but they are wonderfully free of judgment and condemnation about this information. (Infallible people have nothing to be defensive about.) Most splendid of all, eccentrics are never deterred or dismayed by the presence of information contradictory to their convictions, and they do not know the meaning of "defeat." Defeat, in the eccentric's view, is simply an altered course of adaptation. Don Quixote, convinced of the rightness of his cause, was not eccentric because he tilted at windmills, but because he refused to stop. Being Don Quixote, what else could he do? No tilting at windmills, no Don Quixote.

Eccentricity is one of the more charming modes of subversion, because eccentrics usually do not see themselves as such. Often they judge themselves to be quite ordinary. What they cannot see, and what we are indebted to them for, is that they elevate the ordinary to the Ordinary without even trying, the lower case to the capital in a glide. Just by being who they are, by refusing to fall prey to any collective insistence on conformity of attitude, they unconsciously maintain a subversive stance which throws things off balance. Like the small subversive movements of the individual psyche that relishes staring down what others will not look at, that wants to engage those emotions and values that others wish to bury, eccentricity rarely happens on a grand scale. Like the art of the personal, it is also the art of the small. It is mostly visible in the small things people do, the odd ways in which they do usual things.

It should come as no surprise that the age of Queen Victoria – whose very name signifies the epitome of the Ordinary – was also an age of many and marvelous eccentric characters. It seems very fitting, even to be expected, that the Victorian era of social conformity, sexual repression, and moral rectitude, was also the age of characters both imaginal, such as Sherlock Holmes and Ebenezeer Scrooge, and actual, such as Charles Dickens, Charlotte and Emily Brontë, George Eliot (Mary Ann Evans), Charles Darwin, Oscar Wilde, and Jack the Ripper. And these are only a handful of luminaries. It seems equally fitting that the era should close not only with Victoria's death in 1901, but with the birth of Walt Disney. Think of it: within a single year that marked the turn of the century, Friedrich Nietzsche died, the Cakewalk became the most fasionable dance, Fred Astaire was born, and Freud's *Interpretation of Dreams* was published. Adolph Hitler was eleven years old.

Of all the odd characters of Queen Victoria's long reign, my favorite is the Reverend Charles Lutwidge Dodgson, who died in 1898 at the age of sixty-six. He never married, never fathered children, never seems to have traveled outside his native country. He taught mathematics at Christ Church, Oxford, for more than thirty years and dedicated to Queen Victoria a scholarly volume entitled, *An Elementary Treatise on Determinants*. He was known to be occasionally shy but never retiring, stored much of his life in pigeonholes, keeping and cataloguing every piece of correspondence sent or received over a thirty-seven year period, so that there were approximately 98,000 cross-references in his files when he died. He kept seating diagrams and notes on what his guests ate for dinner so as not to serve them the same dish again. He was fastidious in habit and though he lived alone, he corresponded with a broad circle of literary, religious, and political friends, including Lord Salisbury the Prime Minister, Alfred Tennyson, and Christina Rossetti.

The Reverend Mr. Dodgson was easily offended by irreverence in adults about sacred matters, but considered such irreverence the natural and delightful expression of wonder and curiosity and sensibleness in children. When his behavior or motives were criticized, he merely told his critics they were wrong. And though his moral character as a Christian clergyman was impeccable, and his scholarship as a mathematician more than acceptable, he seemed capable of high excitement only when in the company of young girls, whom he photographed in the nude whenever possible.

Dodgson's written works not related to mathematics number more than one thousand pages. His most important contribution to the field of psychology, as I regard it, was written under a pseudonym – the other of his two personalities – and still stands as a masterwork of the faculty of imagination. The title of this is *Alice's Adventures in Wonderland* and *Through the Looking Glass*, by the Charles Dodgson we know as Lewis Carroll. Carroll called the original, shorter version of this work, *Alice's Adventures Underground*. (Perhaps the name was changed to *Wonderland* because of the connotation of subversion, illegality and immorality associated with "underground?")

Dressed in his colorless clerical garb, Charles Dodgson might have receded into the anonymity of history but for two things: he had a passion for the friendship of little girls and seems to have loved no one over the age of twelve; and he had a genius, which flowered in the presence of his young muses, for describing a psychologically subversive imaginal world (which is also a satire of his own Victorian world), in the ostensibly innocent form of children's literature. Fortunately he is remembered for his writing and not his photographs, which, lovely and poignant as they are, in our day would probably land him jail, or at least banned from the Web.

It was Dodgson's great good luck to have lived after the invention of the camera but before the advent of Freud. In his lifetime he could photograph Alice Liddell[2] and her young peers, some of them nude, without the automatic Freudian assumptions of sexual perversity, secret moral vices, hidden malevolence of motives. He destroyed most of his photographic negatives and it is probably just as well: in our neo-Victorian era where all children are required to be absolutely non-sexual and where "touching" of any sort (especially in therapists' offices and classrooms) is almost invariably assumed to be exploitive by the adult and harmful to the child, Dodgson likely would be condemned out of hand. He would be known today as Dodgson the child molestor who gives us grief instead of Lewis Carroll who wrote the *Alice* stories and gave us a gift. Panelists on Larry King's show would endlessly analyze his photography and motives instead of his writing and ideas. Like those who will not watch Woody Allen movies because he married his ex-wife's much younger adopted daughter, no doubt there are those who will not want to read Lewis Carroll anymore because they cannot de-moralize his passion for female children.

But *Alice in Wonderland* doesn't have to do with perversion, it has to do with subversion. It is probably one of the best training manuals for subversive psychological thinking ever written. And Lewis Carroll, himself, as the passionate lover of imagination who lived in the same body as the proper Victorian Charles Dodgson, is one of the best examples of how innately subversive personalities survive: by living the creative, wildly imaginative life underneath the everyday routine of "normal" life. So to get a view from a lower angle and "out of center," let us follow Alice down the rabbit hole to Wonderland.

The wonderful thing about Wonderland is that nothing is at it appears there. If taken literally, or as things *seem* to be, nothing makes any sense. This is exactly how Alice takes it, so of course she cannot understand what is happening to or around her. Lacking a psychological eye, unequipped to see through what is right there in front of her to a deeper possibility, Alice is disoriented, confused, frustrated, and sometimes frightened.

Like those of us who do not understand the basic premises of psychic life, Alice insists on applying the rules of logic, the laws of time and space, the assumed fundamentals of the world above the rabbit hole. That is her familiar world, the world of everyday consciousness, manners, routines, things known and loved. But once down the rabbit hole (which Freud would call a "parapraxis," an unconscious slip of the foot), she leaves all that and enters a realm where subversion is the order of the day, inversion is normal, logic has completely different premises, and Alice, because she doesn't understand any of this, is the only one in Wonderland who doesn't make sense.

Jung would probably say that Alice has met up with the personified creatures that animate psyche. His idea that we are *in* soul, (*esse in anima*) rather than soul being in us, is enormously helpful in negotiating passage through this world. Alice, cast in the role of what we call "ego," has a series of encounters with living characters that function according to laws entirely different – even unnatural – from the way Alice understands the world. These wonderland folk, like Jung's "archetypal images" or "autonomous complexes," come and go and are in shifting relationships with each other in defiance of the physical laws governing time, space, and the trans- formation of matter. Their logic is so perfect that Alice's little mind is quite boggled; she, like us, never grasps the fact that the *premises* of Wonderland logic are different from those she has been taught and has always taken for granted, and so the conclusions feel convincing, but are still incompre- hensible. She tries to understand Wonderland on her own terms. Of course it doesn't work. Alice never grasps the hard fact that in Wonderland "you may have jam yesterday and jam tomorrow, but never jam today."

Alice is a plucky little girl, polite, intelligent, curious, and remarkably able to take care of herself in this craziness. No need for us to worry about coping skills or ego-strength with this mini-Victorian. But she simply does not know how to make her way through Wonderland like a *resident*;

at best she is a mostly lost, half-reluctant tourist. Like most of us, too, she probably thought she *had* a soul, but now she has fallen *into* soul. Though well adapted above-ground, Alice now begins to suffer a variety of symptoms: she might be diagnosed in a psychiatric unit as schizophrenic, because she is disoriented as to time and place and suffers perceived bodily distortion from the cookie she eats which makes her grow taller or smaller. There is also a potion of unknown chemistry she drinks to try to get back to her normal size, an indication that she abuses drugs. And once she starts *talking* to some of the weird characters in Wonderland, she would qualify for a diagnosis of Multiple Personality Disorder. (So much for the harmless innocence of children's literature.)

In this subterranean region of Wonderland, known in modern terms as "the unconscious psyche," all is living, animated image, each distinct with its own character, constantly shifting in relation to other characters in a dimension where time and even space are irrelevant, inapplicable concepts. This world is barely comparable to the one Alice left above ground: usual things are reversed as in a looking glass, usual meanings are subverted in deceptive appearances, contradictory actions, misunder-stood implications, double-bindings. But, as in a mirror, all things here, so reversed, are reflected to infinite depth. And all things here, so sub-verted, lead us deeper into perception of *psychic* reality as we learn to see through the surface appearances of things.

In Wonderland, images and meanings and experiences emerge, take on clarity, and then recede, take form and fade away, like the Cheshire Cat, who can be seen in varying degrees of depth from grin to tail as he chooses to reveal himself. The Wonderland inhabitants, like the Cat, seem to come and go with a purposefulness known only to themselves. To Alice, their activities and talk seem silly, or frightening, or both. She is often called "poor Alice" because she is so often confused and appre-hensive. She, like the part of us that remains a child, is anxious and unsure – she wants to trust and be "centered" in all the constructs of the universe formed above ground. She wants to be grounded in rationality and self-assurance, but these qualities are fragile and thin in Wonderland, and provide neither comfort nor direction. Wonderland is not necessarily or always a place of joy or innocence.

Alice is like the dreamer who finds herself in a dream where she is alone and lost in an unfamiliar city, or who does not understand what is said to her even though each word is clear and distinct and loud. For that matter, she tends to see things in terms of equivalences, one-to-one meanings, this means this, that means that – so that ideas or images or words have only one set of meanings. She is frustrated, not charmed, by ambiguity. Her mind takes in only blacks and whites, no grays, no subtle tones or shadows of varying density.

The trouble is that Alice never comes to see *herself* as an image. She is literal minded, so she takes all the Wonderland creatures literally too. Of course, that is exactly when they make no sense at all. Tweedledee and Tweedledum have the following exchange in the woods with Alice, as they watch the Red King sleeping and snoring:

> "He's dreaming now," said Tweedledee, "and what do you think he's dreaming about?"
>
> Alice said, "Nobody can guess that."
>
> "Why, about *you!*" Tweedledee exclaimed, clapping his hands triumphantly. "And if he left off dreaming about you, where do you suppose you'd be?"
>
> "Where I am now, of course," said Alice.
>
> "Not you!" Tweedledee retorted contemptuously. "You'd be nowhere. Why, you're only a sort of thing in his dream!"
>
> "If that there King was to wake," added Tweedledum, "you'd go out – bang! – just like a candle!"
>
> "I shouldn't!" Alice exclaimed indignantly. "Besides, if *I'm* only a sort of thing in his dream, what are *you*, I should like to know?"
>
> "Ditto," said Tweedledum.
>
> "Ditto, ditto!" cried Tweedledee.
>
> He shouted this so loud that Alice couldn't help saying "Hush! You'll be waking him, I'm afraid, if you make so much noise."
>
> "Well, it's no use *your* talking about waking him," said Tweedledum, "when you're only one of the things in his dream. You know very well you're not real."
>
> "I *am* real!" said Alice, and began to cry.
>
> "You won't make yourself a bit realler by crying," Tweedledee remarked.

The Tweedles are right: the psyche's image-making capability makes us real, generates us as imaginal creatures. When we live in a "dream" we live also in a deeper realm, an additional dimension of meaning below the surface, below the superficial behaviors and activities that give us only partial identities. Alice has trouble absorbing the main lesson of Wonderland: that we are each an image and reflection of a much deeper reality than the ordinary above ground surface world we inhabit. The difference is the difference between Charles Dodgson and Lewis Carroll: two dimensions of the same life.

Wonderland is a place where one finds new ways of perceiving reality, where it is no trouble at all to imagine and enjoy the impossible – because when you imagine something, it is a reality: a metaphorical reality like a poem, not a literal reality like a news story. Look at what happens at the Tea Party Alice attends, along with the Mad Hatter and the incomparable March Hare. They are all seated (with the Dormouse who keeps falling asleep) at the large tea table:

> "Have some wine," the March Hare said in an encouraging tone. Alice looked all around the table, but there was nothing on it but tea. "I don't see any wine," she remarked. "There isn't any," said the March Hare.

The March Hare, who is not limited to actual appearances, is able to perceive things which are invisible to the prosaic eye. This rabbit is enlightened from within with a vision of how things are or could be in the world out there, except that for him, unlike for most of us, "in here" and "out there" are useless – even false – categories. He is not hallucinating, he simply sees from an imaginal perspective, the same way a good photographer "sees" emotion in a subject and gives us not just a "picture" but an "image." The March Hare sees what is invisible to a literal perspective, or you could say that he sees with a third eye. He is not a materialist: his perception is not limited to his five senses. He sees a psychic image, and psychic images have a reality of their own, like invisible wine, and like dreams. And true to the logic of the imagination, the March Hare can extend an invitation to "have some wine" simultaneously with his charming assent that "there isn't any," putting the more literal-minded Alice in a confusing, apparently illogical, contradiction. She is herself an image of the archetypal literalist and materialist in each of us. The March Hare, afer all, is a native of Wonderland and speaks from its point of view, while Alice, poor Alice, is merely a visitor who doesn't speak the language very well. One could legitimately ask which of them is the eccentric.

Diane Arbus, American photographer, disturbed, eccentric, brilliant with a camera, would have felt at home in Wonderland, even though actual "home" for Arbus was not a happy place. Her psychological profile would have filled more than the usual number of intake forms at any psychotherapy clinic. Her symptoms included a narcissistic wound, features of histrionic and borderline personality disorders, and recurring major affective disorder in the form of depression. She committed suicide at the age of forty-eight by opening her wrists in her bathtub. With this information, however, we know nothing of the real Diane Arbus.

Arbus can also be described as a woman who took photographs of people whose reality helped her give substance to her own. Using her camera as an imaginal third eye, she had a spiritual affinity with the March Hare, who invites Alice to drink invisible wine. Arbus once said, "It's very subtle and a little embarrassing to me, but I really believe there are things which nobody would see unless I photographed them."[3] She found the deepest images of her reality right in front of her walking around New York City, and sometimes in dark rabbit-like holes she was afraid to fall into but did anyway. She saw herself in the people she photographed, came to fascinating and disturbing recognitions in them. She photographed the "freaks" and the "strange" – nudists, dwarves, transvestites – all the "characters" who populate a kind of wonderland, but which can only be called freakish, strange, abnormal, from an above ground point of view.

If you want to know Diane Arbus in her reality, look at her photographs. She was always looking for a confirmation of her reality, her experience.

> One of the things I felt I suffered from as a kid was I never felt adversity. I was confirmed in a sense of unreality which I could only feel as unreality. And the sense of being immune was, ludicrous as it seems, a painful one. It was as if I didn't inherit my own kingdom for a long time. The world seemed to me to belong to the world. I could learn things but they never seemed to be my own experience."[4]

Arbus's work as a photographer was an attempt to make herself real – possibly much like what Charles Dodgson tried to do, making himself real through the imagination of "Lewis Carroll" and bringing fresh life to his Victorian soul through the creation of Wonderland. Diane Arbus would have easily understood Tweedledee's observation that Alice is just a sort of thing in someone else's dream, and the Cheshire Cat's reassuring comment to Alice that "we're all mad here." While Arbus was photographing nudists – not the colonies, but the nudists – she said, "it's a little bit like walking into an hallucination without being quite sure whose it is."[5] Her work has tremendous depth and power to move us emotionally because she never let her fear of her subjects interefere with her profound respect for them. Her subjects are always honored in her photographs by her honesty, her refusal to lie about them or make them more or less or other than they are. She does not control their reality, makes no attempt to discredit or distort whatever image presents itself. She said, "I work from awkwardness. By that I mean I don't like to arrange things. If I stand in front of something, instead of arranging it, I arrange myself."[6]

Alice would have felt better in Wonderland had she been given this advice.

_____

"Wonderland" is disturbing because it defies our cherished notions of reality and logic. Some of Wonderland's creatures are not only a bit demented, like the Red Queen who runs around hysterically screaming "Off with their heads!" Some appear to be downright psychopathic, like the Walrus, who is capable of a most carnivorous, sinister seduction of innocent little oysters.

> . . . The Walrus and the Carpenter
>   Walked on a mile or so,
> And then they rested on a rock
>   Conveniently low:
> And all the little Oysters stood
>   And waited in a row . . .
>
> "A loaf of bread," the Walrus said,
>   "Is what we chiefly need:
> Pepper and vinegar besides
>   Are very good indeed –
> Now, if you're ready, Oysters dear,
>   We can begin to feed."
>
> "But not on us!" the Oysters cried,
>   Turning a little blue.
> "After such kindness, that would be
>   A dismal thing to do!". . .
>
> "It seems a shame," the Walrus said
>   "To play them such a trick.
> After we've brought them out so far,
>   And made them trot so quick!" . . .
>
> "O Oysters," said the Carpenter,
>   "You've had a pleasant run!
> Shall we be trotting home again?"
>   But answer came there none –
> And this was scarcely odd, because
>   They'd eaten every one.

Wonderland destroys any idea we might have of psychological orderli-ness, predictability, balance. Things are always turning the wrong way, carrying Alice (our ego-selves) to extremes, heaping confusions upon puzzlements. Each of the Wonderland characters knows only its own way of perceiving its world, its own one-sided way of being. The Cheshire Cat appears and disappears but never leaves its tree. The White Rabbit is always on the run because he is always late. Humpty Dumpty just sits on the wall and arrogantly pontificates to Alice.

So Wonderland has something to teach us about one-sidedness and being off balance. Wonderland, as one image of what the unconscious psyche "looks" like, is a training ground for subversion of over-valued conscious notions.

The idea of "eccentricity," being out of center and somewhat off balance, naturally constellates fantasies and ideas of "centredness" and "balance." So while we continue walking with the Walrus and Carpenter along the briny beach, it seems worthwhile to revisit Jung's idea of the "Self" in terms of the modern quest for "balance," placing both against the exquisite logic of Wonderland, which works subversively against the collectively popular fantasy of "balance."

In most psychology books (especially books about Jungian psycho-logy), when you see a drawing of the "structure of the psyche," it is a circle. The psyche is imagined to be round, like the earth or the sun (or nearly round, like an oyster). The circumference is what Jung called the "Self," distinguishing it from the "ego" by giving it a capital "S" because it refers to the totality of the psyche, not only to the relatively small field of ego-centered consciousness. The centerpoint of the circle is also the Self, the center of the totality.

This is a very comforting diagram. Circles offer containment, safety, a ruddy roundness, wagons in a protective formation to keep the enemy outside. But our colloquial language also betrays a profound dislike and distrust of circles. This quintessential symbol of "wholeness," in which we imagine things are well "balanced" in contained quadrants, is also an image of madness, deviousness, or frustration: going in circles, being in a spin, spinning your wheels, talking in circles, beating around a bush, circular reasoning; and sometimes a circle is downright vicious. We much prefer things straight: straight talk going right to the point; straight sex; honest straight shooting; going straight after prison; the fast, efficient straight line as shortest distance between two points; and the straight protects against moral deviation because it is narrow.

But you recall from your geometry class that there isn't *really* a circle or a centerpoint, because the dots that make it up don't have any dimension – they are hypothetical concepts just as the "Self" is a hypothetical concept, and it, too, doesn't literally exist. But even if called by another name or no name at all, most of us, and Jungians in particular, *love* this concept, elevate it, strive for it, and dream about it, and if you strive for it long enough and draw enough mandalas, you begin to think there really is such a thing as a Self, capital S, and that it is located on the other end of the axis from the Ego, which we also take to be real, ignoring Tweedledee and Tweedledum's observation that we aren't real at all. And crying over the loss of this conceptual ideal won't make us or it a bit realler.

It has always seemed to me that this concept of the Self as the center or in the center is a defense against the chaos and nowhereness of psychic reality. As the digressive talk of the Walrus about cabbages and kings is meant to distract the little oysters from the realization that they are about to be eaten, maybe the idea of psyche having a center is a distraction from the realization that it does not. It is just at this point that the possibility of eccentricity may rescue us from the fantasy of "balance," taking us out of the well-measured and quadrated circle, out of the viciousness of the circle that keeps us circling round an illusion that we are following a wonderland road to the psychic utopia of individuation. We should probably pay attention to the observation of the Red Queen, with whom Alice can barely keep up as they run at top speed.

> The most curious part of the thing was, that the trees and the other things round them never changed their places at all: however fast they went, they never seemed to pass anything. . . .
>
> Alice . . . was getting so much out of breath: and still the Queen cried "Faster! Faster!" and dragged her along. "Are we nearly there?" Alice managed to pant out at last.
>
> "Nearly there!" the Queen repeated. "Why, we passed it ten minutes ago! Faster!" And they ran on . . .
>
> . . . Suddenly, just as Alice was getting quite exhausted, they stopped, and she found herself sitting on the ground, breathless and giddy. . . .
>
> Alice looked round her in great surprise. "Why, I do believe we've been under this tree the whole time! Everything's just as it was!"
>
> "Of course it is," said the Queen. "What would you have it?"
>
> "Well, in *our* country," said Alice, still panting a little, "you'd generally get to somewhere else – if you ran very fast for a long time as we've been doing."
>
> "A slow sort of country!" said the Queen. "Now, *here*, you see, it takes all the running *you* can do, to keep in the same place. If you

want to get somewhere else, you must run at least twice as fast as that!"

So much for trying to get to somewhere imagined as balanced or centered or whole or individuated. And running is very hard on the knees.

There is no "center" in Wonderland, only a series of movements from place to place, and a series of encounters among assorted psychic figures. If there *is* a center – and following Lewis Carroll's love of mathematical order and symmetry, there is a *sort* of center – it is right in the middle of Alice's adventures. This is the middle chapter, the halfway point: going to the center in Wonderland takes you to the Mad Tea Party. This is the very place Alice was not at all sure she wanted to go. Shortly after she arrives in Wonderland she meets the Cheshire Cat, who gives very good insight into what the place is like and, by comparison, what Alice is like. She asks him,

> "Would you tell me, please, which way I ought to go from here?"
> "That depends a good deal on where you want to get to," said the Cat.
> "I don't much care where –" said Alice.
> "Then it doesn't matter which way you go," said the Cat.
> "– so long as I get *somewhere*," Alice added as an explanation.
> "Oh, you're sure to do that," said the Cat, "if you only walk long enough."
> Alice felt that this could not be denied, so she tried another question. "What sort of people live about here?"
> "In *that* direction," the Cat said, waving its right paw round, "lives a Hatter: and in *that* direction," waving the other paw, "lives a March Hare. Visit either you like: they're both mad."
> "But I don't want to go among mad people," Alice remarked.
> "Oh, you can't help that," said the Cat: "we're all mad here. I'm mad. You're mad."
> "How do you know I'm mad?" said Alice.
> "You must be," said the Cat, "or you wouldn't have come here."

In Wonderland, all premise of order, of how things should be, break down. And in the center of this breakdown of order is madness, delightfully epitomized by that most English of institutions, the tea party. In Wonderland, in dreamland, fantasyland, Disneyland, the unconscious, the underworld, "the center" signifies breakdown, confusion, reversal, madness, and a backward logic that will break your mind if you resist it. Put another way: when you think in terms of *the* center, you are mad. For Alice, the mad tea party in particular, and Wonderland in general, is an experience of W.B. Yeats's observation that "Things fall apart; the center cannot hold." The center cannot hold *in* Wonderland, nor *for* it; and if it cannot hold, then let it go.

By living some of the deeper aspects of life out of center, off center, off balance, at the edge, one lives subversively, turning under beloved ideals of being balanced and centered. The central values of a culture need constantly to be approached with a subversive attitude, lest they become the fixed centerpoint of collective life and thus impose themselves as ideals on individuals, the quickest way to destroy individuality. If we were all to become well balanced, who would notice where our individual craziness and chaos and eccentricity is?

The conceptual ideal of the Self as center of the psyche is a defensive illusion against what Hillman has best described as the polycentric nature of the psyche.[7] Psyche has many centers; each of your complexes is a complete universe of meaning, a riddle with an archetype at *its* center. We are never free from this or that complex, never free of all archetypal perspectives – even the Self is an archetypal idea, and then only one among many. But, except in moments of mystical rapture, the experience of totality, wholeness, completeness, is *not* part of our daily psychological experience, and there is no special reason why it should be. Psychic life is not lived exclusively on mountain peaks. The experience of being in confusion, emotional disarray, nowheresville, out of whack, off center, is much closer to our realities, much closer to how it really is with us, and is the sure and certain sign that we are alive.

And here is the most compelling reason to abandon the idea of being "balanced" and "centered," because to be at the center, dead center, is to be dead. The point of balance is the still point, the point where you are fixated, where nothing moves. Freud was correct to consider fixation as a pathological condition associated with immaturity or arrested development: such a condition of motionlessness is death to psyche. *Eccentricity, being out of center, as a mode of subverting centrist fantasies, is a mode of survival.*

It says on Lewis Carroll's tombstone that he "fell asleep," and in his case, maybe this is not a euphemism. Charles Dodgson died, Lewis Carroll fell asleep, into an endless dream. Alice eventually woke up from her long adventurous dream in Wonderland, but she was changed by it. And as it was with Alice, maybe so it should be with us: there ought to be something different about us after we fall into Wonderland and wake up. Perhaps our characters could be a bit more sharply defined, there ought to be a wonderment that we might be figures in another's dream, maybe we could be a little more courageous when we fall into new rabbit holes. I don't think consciousness means being centered or in a carefully arranged balance or getting out of Wonderland; I think it means being able to see the Wonderland dimension of life even when we're awake. Like Alice after she woke up, when our eyes are open we ought not to be too absolutely sure which is the dream and which is the reality. This may be the most subversive attitude of all.

To return (full circle, as it were) to the beginning, the question remains as to whether pigs have wings, which, as far as I know, they don't, but perhaps some future pig will figure out how to fly anyway. I don't know why the sea is boiling hot, so I leave that to the oceanographers.

Notes

1. Edith Sitwell, *English Eccentrics*, New York: The Vanguard Press, 1957, p. 21.
2. The real Alice Liddell, Carroll's heroine, bears no resemblance to John Tenniel's famous illustrations, but actually looks like a dark-haired young *femme fatale*, beautiful and older than her years. Looking at Dodgson's lovely photographic portrait of her, one can see the archetypal figure of that Victorian obsession, *la belle dame sans merci*, even in such an obviously child's face and demeanor. Morton Cohen's biography of Dodgson (*Lewis Carroll: A Biography*, Knopf, 1995) documents that nearly every man who met the young Alice fell in love with her, and that only the intervention of Queen Victoria herself prevented one of the royal princes from pursuing marriage to her.
3. Doon Arbus and Marvin Israel (eds), *Diane Arbus*, New York: Aperture Monographs, 1972, p. 15.
4. Ibid., p. 5.
5. Ibid., p. 4.
6. Ibid., p. 12.
7. This is one of the principal themes of James Hillman's *Re-Visioning Psychology*, New York: Harper & Row, 1975.

Chapter 2

Feeding the psyche
Junk words and corn-fed music

Even though speech comes out of the mouth and into the ear, it needs to be perceived through the eye. We have to look at what we are saying, not merely hear it as ordinary communication but as implication for how the psyche is faring as we articulate it. Our daily language, the speech we use to talk to each other and to ourselves, needs to be examined because the subversiveness of words leads down and into a deeper realm of hidden meanings. The eyes have ears too. As we must learn to "see in the dark," so we must learn to hear meaning in echoes of language, which is the daily currency of our exchange.

Our culture is profoundly ambivalent about words. The sayings we use express both a distrust and an honoring of words. Sticks and stones may break my bones but words will never harm me. Eat your words. (You are what you eat.) Your word is your bond. She's as good as her word. Actions speak louder than words. Don't do as I do, do as I say. Put in a good word for me. And, for Christians, the Word is God himself. Our ambivalence about words points to the power they have to make or break us. They are one of the fundamental ways we develop trust in others, and a means by which we form our self-images. And they are also ephemeral, insubstantial air, signifying nothing. One picture is worth a thousand of them.

But words *are* pictures, images formed from language rather than from paint or clay or film. *Psyche*, for example, means both "soul" and "butterfly" in Greek; when the Greeks *say* "psyche" they *see* "butterfly." The soul looks like a butterfly. The word gives substance, through image, to the concept. In this language, we can see what the psyche looks like: a butterfly, richly colored in more varieties and patterns than can be counted, hard to catch, beautiful in its own right, forever trying to evade the dominant culture's restrictive net, fluttering mightily and with surprising determination in search of some kind of realization that begins with caterpillar-like crawling and ends flying free.

Of course, "psyche" is not a "thing" at all, not a literal mass that can be quantitatively measured. "Psyche" is the perspective or lens through which we look at all aspects of life: it isn't *what* we see, it's *how* we see. It isn't only *what* we hear, it's *how* we hear. It's not only the object of our psychotherapeutic tinkering but also the subject which does the tinkering. "Psyche" is a metaphor for depth, for meaning, for that which makes connections, for the capacity of our species to "turn events into experiences."[1]

Since psyche is not a literal thing, we can only speak of it in metaphors: it is *like* a butterfly, like a drop of quicksilver, like a circle, like a beautiful woman. Psyche's language is metaphorical language; metaphor is the psyche's mother tongue. Psychic life thrives or starves depending largely on the words we use, what words we feed ourselves, what word pictures we paint to portray ourselves and our experiences.

Patriarchal culture is hostile to psychic life because its words are only of the mind, without body, without substance, intangible, immaterial – that is, supremely abstract and full of air. Its language, which is common currency in our daily lives, is less able to portray our experience than visual mediums, particularly television, but also movies, theater, photography, painting, sculpture. In an age when words are being processed faster than thought, the soul is starved for words that speak of us, for us, about us, and to us, that make audible and articulate statements of who we are and what we are about.

In Latin, *articulus* means "joint," or "limb." Referring to words, it means to join distinct parts or links into a coherent whole. In a world where *numbers* increasingly determine reality (stock market quotes, statistical measurements, demographic charts, social security numbers, cholesterol readings, and on and on), it becomes critically important to reclaim the power of precise speech – not only for political reasons, but because it is the first and perhaps most important act on behalf of psyche. The conscious articulating of ourselves is how we become clear and whole persons, and how we recognize individual distinctiveness.

In 1949 George Orwell published the novel *1984*, portraying a dismal society in which people were absolutely controlled in their thought and behavior by the reduction of words. The language of that futuristic society was called "Newspeak," and its intention was to "make speech . . . as nearly as possible independent of consciousness."[2] The idea wasn't so much to *subvert* thought as to *eliminate* it, by depleting the meaning of words and reducing the number of words available. The whole language consisted of one-syllable words, a few prefixes and suffixes, words purged of all ambiguity, complexity, and ambivalence. It required little, if any, thought – only reflexive automatic responses. For example, the word "good" still existed, but "bad," which independently carries a whole set of categories and associations, was unnecessary: you said "ungood." Categories of "better" and "best" were also unnecessary; you said, "good, gooder, goodest." Words suggesting forbidden heretical ideas – such as *justice, freedom, honor* – fell into categories called "oldthink" and "crimethink." Since these ideas and images could not be spoken, eventually, they could not be thought. "Ultimately," wrote Orwell, "it was hoped to make articulate speech issue from the larynx without involving the higher brain centers at all. This aim was frankly admitted in the Newspeak word *duckspeak*, meaning 'to quack like a duck,'"[3] and was used as a word of praise if the speaker quacked out orthodox opinions. To call someone a *doubleplusgood duckspeaker* was a warm compliment. Three obvious modern examples of good duckspeakers are Jerry Falwell, Dr. Laura, and George W. Bush. (Dan Quayle was a doubleplusgood duckspeaker.) But there are many politicians and psychotherapists who are gooder and goodest duckspeakers as well.

The language of modern popular psychology has become the Newspeak of our daily lives. Much of the way we talk is not of a New Age but Newspeak, Orwellian style. This is why I believe in the devil, even though I'm a nice Jewish girl from Brooklyn. I believe in the devil because I hear him everywhere – he's a Newspeaking sweet-talker, just as he was in the garden of Eden, and he lives in our language. He is not the clichéd, ugly red devil of Christian tradition. The devil I'm talking about isn't even evil – he is merely hollow, like many of our words. He creates the illusion of depth and significance in words that have neither. He puts nice words in our mouths so that we don't notice our hunger for, and absence of, not-nice, high-protein words. He gives us mass-produced, one-dimensional simplistic words.

This is why I'm not "sharing" anything with you here. Instead, I'm telling you what I think. "Share" is a nice word but it has a shadow, and it means that whoever is sharing is giving only a part, not the whole. Something shared also means a part withheld; the word is less generous than it sounds. And it is too often used as a moralistic weapon, implicitly obligating whoever is on the receiving end to accept what is "shared," or risk appearing to be arrogant, aloof, anti-social, ungood.

The devil is a hard-core right-wing literalist and is the enemy of metaphor, imagination, romance, and real, plain, emotion. The language of modern psychology has become, for many of us, the language of our daily lives, and it is the devil's native tongue. It is our current version of Orwell's Newspeak, a devilish way of making speech as nearly as possible independent of consciousness.

Now, the devil is not stupid. He knows, as Adrienne Rich once wrote, that a thinking woman sleeps with monsters. So if the devil can persuade us to keep our mouths shut or to use words which sound good but are harmless and empty, nothing need change. The *status quo*, both individually and collectively, is maintained, and eventually psyche atrophies from stagnancy, boredom, or despair. But I can tell you, what the devil most fears is this: if women ever bring the fullness of our emotional and spiritual power and authority to consciousness, continental plates will split apart and reshape the face and core of the planet and the Great Mother Earth will have so many splendid multiple orgasms that she will shift on her axis.

Ah, but the devil is very subtle and cunning: he presents himself sweetly in attractive guises, such as quick-fix therapies and simplistic how-to books with titles like *30 Days to Happiness*, *Getting Better*, and *Creating Choices: How Adult Children Can Turn Today's Dreams Into Tomorrow's Reality*. (Visit your local bookstore.) The devil speaks in moderate, inoffensive tones designed to lull us into feeling comfortable and feeling good. He persuades us to raise the inflection at the end of sentences so that every statement becomes a tentative question, every pronouncement an uncertainty. Of course we are rendered insecure and anxious. He appeals to our need for safety when he has us speak words that do not challenge or invite risk or offer softness. And he is a non-extremist protector of the norm: by putting innocuous words in our mouths, he protects us from accusations of being *too* strident, *too* aggressive, *too* angry. His greatest joy is in deception, and his preferred mode of deception is in speech, getting us to use a lot of nice words to say little of importance. This is why psychology has become the devil's playground: he has sucked out the vitality, imaginal quality, and metaphorical resonance from psychology's language, run off with the peanuts and left us shells – words that make the language I call *mentalspeak*.

Mentalspeak is a language of the patriarchal mind. It is *not* psychobabble, not unintelligible gibberish. Mentalspeak is far more insidious; it forces us to address each other as partial beings, only mind to mind, as if we had no bodies, no souls, no spirits. If you watch *Star Trek: The Next Generation*, you know that the character Data is an android who can only speak mentalspeak because he is only mind. And because he's not really human and we don't expect him to be, his mentalspeaking is rather endearing and often funny. But his inability to use metaphorical speech and irony makes him a pure example of abstract, conceptual mentalspeak. In one episode Dr. Crusher is teaching him to dance, telling him to do a number of things at once: "Now Data," she says, holding him as a partner, "you lead, like this: right hand here, left hand here; look up, not at your feet, and smile." And Data, concentrating on making all these movements, says very seriously, "This is a very complex set of variables to coordinate, Doctor." As Data learns to make these complex variables come together in a series of steps, he can say precisely what he is doing in his purely conceptual, mentalspeak language. But he can't really *dance*, or say what dancing *is*, because, as a blind woman I once met who played blues piano at a Dallas bar would have said, "he ain't got no rhythm in his bones." And that woman, whose piano could speak far more eloquently than most scholars I've heard, ain't speakin' mentalspeak.

Mentalspeak is a language of mental concepts and abstractions, a father-tongue of analytical definitions. It is hard not to be seduced by abstract mentalspeak words such as *co-dependency*, *issue*, *growth*, and *intimacy*. Like Orwell's Newspeak, mentalspeak is a language "as nearly as possible independent of consciousness," keeping us from knowing *precisely* what we're talking about – not by reducing the number of words, but by inventing words that sound significant but don't carry much meaning. Some words have been merely inflated and had starch added to them, such as the plain word "use," which has been tripled in length to "utilize," even though it means the same thing. Mentalspeak words have neither the weight of matter nor the depth of soul; most mentalspeak words just don't *matter*, they are *im*material to what needs to be said.

Take, for instance, the qualitative difference in the sound of the word *homosexual* and the word *lesbian*. "Homosexual" is a mentalspeak word, coined by a German physician in 1869 referring to an arbitrary category of sexual behavior. It has no sensual resonance in the ear nor appreciable taste on the tongue. "Gay" is a better word because it has a history and multiple meanings, and I think "lesbian" is an even richer word – if you're lucky enough to be female – because it's a strong, solid word, and right there in the very beginning of it are lively sound-images of *l*over, *l*usty, and *l*aughter.

Because most mentalspeak words have no matter and don't matter, we have to try to begin speaking in a mother-tongue of images, substances, metaphorical descriptions, in words that have weight and body, that come *from* the body as supreme metaphor: words that have heat from the blood, that have the salt and smell of tears and sweat, words that we can stomach and that come from the heart.

Psychology has become not only the devil's playground, but also his kitchen, where he cooks up a diet of words that are distasteful or too sweet, bad for the heart, that clog the arteries, aren't seasoned properly, and that have a lot of calories but little nutritional value for the soul. Here are some more mentalspeak junk-food words: *addiction, dysfunctional, relationship, boundary, depression, personal growth, abuse, wellness, wholeness, positive, negative, appropriate, sexuality, spirituality.* These are all imprecise, immaterial concept-words, flat, tasteless and without color. We serve them up as a sort of mental fast-food (goodest duckspeak) so that when we speak to each other, we have a rough idea of what is being said. But shorthand, valuable though it is sometimes, is not prose, and it remains unclear to both speaker and listener just what is *meant* below the surface sounds.

Mentalspeak words cannot be heard through the senses or resonate in the body because they have no body: they are concepts, not living images. How heavy is my depression? How thick is your boundary and what is its texture? What does wellness smell like? There is a difference between saying, as the country-western song does, "I fall to pieces each time I see you again," and, "I regress to psychotic dissociation each time I see you again." It's not a matter of thinking before you speak, but of thinking about what you say. And no one needs a Ph.D. in English to speak of soul matters; some of the best poets and makers of metaphor are, after all, young children.

As adults, we need to consume fewer steroid-loaded words that have false muscle and get on a diet of complex-carbohydrate words, words with high fiber content that are also rich in flavor, that can be chewed over and digested, words that move the bowels. These are substantial words that carry real weight, words whose meaning is immediately understood because they are perceptible through the senses, the body's imagination.

Consider the mentalspeak word, "issue." "Issue" is an all-purpose word that has replaced several other words, such as *dilemma, conflict, quandary, confusion, mess.* The word came into vogue beyond its political usage several years ago, and I have been trying to remember: what did people have before they had issues? How did we talk to each other about our blind confusions, heart-stopping fears, sweet hopes, crippling losses, and hot-blooded enthusiasms before we started calling everything an "issue?" I saw an advertisement in one of my local newspapers a few weeks ago offering counseling for "grief issues," and I wondered: what if I only had the grief, and not the issue?

It was not enough that we obliterated precision and distinction; we then distanced ourselves even further from the real, immediate *emotion* by having issues "around" things. Having an "issue around" abandonment or anger or intimacy is a way of disembodying the soul, a way of dividing the precise experience from the word used to convey it. Much easier to have the issue around the emotion than the emotion itself.

No doubt this is why we are eternally "getting in touch with" whatever we have an issue around, because mentalspeak words distance us from our deeper selves. Unable to touch the heart of the matter, to speak the matter itself, we are always *en route*, getting in touch with, calling long distance to find out how we are. But we ought to shop for words that give the best value for the money – the best, most precise expression of what we want to say. These top-value words are expensive – they cost time, and emotional and intellectual honesty – and they are not discounted.

Most mentalspeak words deny or minimize *depth, complexity*, and *intensity of feeling*. They serve to anesthetize the soul, dull the spirit and keep the mind blank. The over-valuation we give to being "comfortable" makes us more susceptible to disembodied mentalspeak exactly because it is comfortable speech and demands nothing of us. Mentalspeak's preferred mode of expression is to put painful emotions into the passive voice. If I say, "I have a lot of anger," I can have my anger and never have to *be angry*. The active voice is far more threatening than the passive voice – and the active voice is just that, actively moving us to a means of expression that embodies the feeling and fleshes out the experience. When all of me is actively engaged, I don't have an issue around anger – I am mad as hell, I am in a towering rage, I am a Vesuvian eruption, I am a hurricane about to smash your coastline, *take cover!* Mentalspeak numbs our psyches partly through the excessively high value we place on feeling comfortable (which contradicts what we are told about the importance of taking risks) and the high value we give to behaving appropriately (doing the proper thing, which usually means just being conventional).

For the sake of comfort we may use mild words to minimize harsh reality, as in, "I'm not really comfortable with the idea of genocide." And to avoid appearing judgmental we tend to think of "behavior" – another mentalspeak word – as merely appropriate or inappropriate, not in strong categories that state our ethical values and character judgments ("he acts like a coward," "she's fair-minded," "he has a loyal heart").

The mentalspeak word "co-dependency" is the devil's delight. It is such an over-used and all-embracing word that it is practically a generic describing anybody who needs anything. We are addicted to the word "co-dependent." At this point let me remind you that there's a country song which says bluntly, "*I'm crazy for cryin', crazy for tryin,' and I'm crazy for lovin' you.*" Now, we all know what "crazy" means when used this way, but can you imagine using terms like "co-dependency" with a steady bass rhythm and sad guitar? How can we talk legitimately about psychological or emotional necessities without inviting a "diagnosis" of co-dependency? How can we talk seriously and with gravity about passion, about unrequited love, about consuming desire, about betrayal and lust and jealousy, when all these profound movements of the soul are now symptoms of a disorder? How can the individual normalcy of need, or love, or grief, be understood, if their mere existence implies pathology? Don't we experience these emotions with compelling urgency? Or do we really believe that the sheer depth and intractability of our need is proof that we are sick?

If we are to find a vocabulary that begins to express the fullness of our lives, we may have to stop looking to the Father who creates merely by speaking the disembodied, desexualized Word, and start looking to the Matrix, which is our sexual body, with its sensate imagination. The words we use to articulate ourselves profoundly affect our attitudes about the selves we articulate; so we need to notice how we talk and where our words come from. I am convinced we will not find the words we need in the vocabularies of masculinized Western institutions. With one exception: there is country music. Outrageously sexist and heterosexist as most country music is, it has one great, overriding, redeeming feature: *it tells it like it is*. It's corn-fed, home-grown, and builds strong psychic bones and muscles. If you want to speak more or less academically, mentalspeak is a serviceable vocabulary. But if you want words that come from the heart and feed the soul, the menu of lyrics from country-western music and country rock is the place to go. If k.d. lang sings it, one or two servings a day meets my nutritional daily requirement.

Are you coming out of a broken love relationship? Are you telling yourself, or being told, that you have an issue around insecurity, are working through co-dependency needs, and this can be, after all, a positive growth experience? Okay. But let me ask again: did your lover do you wrong? Then tell the devil to go to hell with his mentalspeak, turn up the volume on a Connie Francis record and get into revenge: "*Who's sorry now? Who's sorry now? Who's heart is aching for breaking each vow? Who's sad and blue? Who's crying too – just like I cried over you? You had your way, now you must pay, I'm **glad** that you're sorry now!*" Then, when you're really into a jealous rage, belt out those immortal words of truth: "*You're cheatin' heart will make you weep, you'll cry and cry and try to sleep, but sleep won't come the whole night through, your miserable low-down good-for-nothin' cheatin' heart will tell on you!*"

Maybe you need re-parenting but don't want your inner child to dictate your dependency needs, and perhaps you're confused about whether you're an adult, a child, or an adult child. There are probably so many issues surrounding these that you don't even know what your main issue is, but there are songs and lyrics with the right rhythm that can bring you in and express the exact feeling: "*Hold me close, hold me tight, make me thrill with delight 'cause I die every time we're apart. I want you, I need you, I love you, with all my heart.*"

If you're feeling sexually deprived and don't know the appropriate way to come on to someone – there is no "appropriate" way – you can get psyched up by singing, "*Oh darlin', how I'd love to lay you down, lay you down and softly whisper pretty love words in your ear.*" It's sure more to the point than saying something like, "Hi, I don't mean to be disrespectful of your boundaries but if you feel it's appropriate I would be comfortable being sexual with you."

Wouldn't you rather hear someone say, "*I'll love you til the roses forget to bloom, until the twelfth of never,*" instead of, "I've processed my feelings and I'm ready to make a commitment" – which could also mean readiness to put you into a psychiatric unit.

Perhaps someone has spoken mentalspeak to you recently, something like, "I've been processing my thoughts and feelings surrounding the issues I have around my relationship with you, and you need to know that I've chosen to share my intimate space by being sexual with you. But setting boundaries is scary." Now, you may or may not have understood more or less what was said. But wouldn't it have thrilled you and made you gurgle if it came out this way: "*If I said you had a beautiful body would you hold it against me? If I said you were an angel would you treat me like the devil tonight?*"

Of course, like all of us, I want my lover to take responsibility for her feelings and decisions. I would love her even if she told me in mentalspeak that she's basically shame-based from a dysfunctional family and has an issue around self-esteem. And she would probably love me even if I told her in mentalspeak that I have a lot of denial surrounding abandonment issues and I would have a lot of anger if she didn't keep her commitment. But I'd much rather that she sang to me, "*I keep a close watch on this heart of mine, I keep my eyes wide open all the time,*" and I could respond with, "*I keep the end out for the tie that binds, because you're mine I walk the line.*"

Since mentalspeak is a mind-language, it tends to keep us in the mind only, decapitated, above and on the surface of life. But metaphors and word-pictures take us deeper into psyche where image is the language of the soul. Country music is every bit as neurotic as the culture it reflects, but its lyrics often go to the heart of the matter because they don't speak of concepts, but of life and how it feels to be loved or lost, enraged, ecstatic, or forgotten. Language does not have to be complicated in order to have a therapeutic effect and express complex ideas; it has to give substance to our complexes and enable us to speak imagistically about them.

There was a time when a woman could experience overwhelming passion and lust and a strong, dark desire to possess the beloved and to be possessed – and could understand this as a natural movement of life. I worry that those women who are true daughters of Aphrodite and Artemis – goddesses of love and the hunt – have become dependent for their definition of psychological health on a simplistic psychology that disallows extremeness, as if extremeness is by definition pathological. The message is that when we are in any sort of extremis we are sick. Thus we too often mistake depth of passion for addiction, legitimate need for dependency, wholeness for feeling good. The seduction of mentalspeak is that it's easy to use; the danger of using it is that it makes it harder for us to see and feel through to the real bottom of things.

Mentalspeak aggravates the internal conflicts we all go through. A vocabulary of psychoterms that implies what is sick and how to be healthy *increases* stress and anxiety because it gives us abstract generalized words which we then try to apply to our own personal conditions, whether they fit or not. We tend to become like what we are diagnosed or described, just as persons and groups tend to take on the qualities consistently projected on to them. From a tiny nubbin grows a huge hook. How often does the term "co-dependency" make us mute with fear that what we truly feel is sick because we've been told it's sick, because it has entered the vocabulary as a sickness, an addiction? Wouldn't it be wonderful if just for a moment you could throw the mentalspeak word out and all therapeutic caution aside and tell your heart's true love: "*All of me, why not take all of me? Can't you see I'm no good without you? . . . How can I go on living without you? You took the part that once was my heart, so why not take all of me?*" Of course I want and need to make life choices independently, wisely, deliberately. But it is also true, as Connie Francis sang time and again, that "*my heart has a mind of its own, I'm a puppet and I just can't seem to break the string. Somehow I can't dismiss the memory of his kiss. Yes, my heart has a mind of its own.*" Country-western lyrics express a rawness that is much closer to the truth of how our lives really are than bloodless mentalspeak words. "*Four walls to hear me*" can be a room of my own or just four walls closing in on me. How you sing these words gives nuance to the experience of independence, for example. Independence, even when possible, is not all it's cracked up to be, and sometimes is used as a euphemism for loneliness. Nor is there any way any of us is going to get through life without frequently looking ridiculous – not to mention inappropriate. The song says, "*everybody's somebody's fool, and there are no exceptions to the rule.*" And being a romantic fool myself, I could never bring myself to say that I wanted to "be sexual." I would have to stupidly croon words like, "*Lay your head upon my pillow, lay your warm and tender body close to mine.*" I don't know what "being sexual" means, but I do know a warm and tender body when I want one.

Mentalspeak reflects our culture's schizophrenic split between mind and body, between sex and religion, splits we all suffer from in varying degrees. Mentalspeak perpetuates those splits by not including the language of the body and the physicality of words. It does not help us repair the self-divided condition with which we enter the world, still less as we enter the male world as girl-children, because a conceptual language of generalities cannot fully articulate subjective experience, individually perceived truth, or the wordless hunger of the human soul for dignity and meaning. I believe that those of us who have been denied the credibility of our subjective experience, and with it the dignity and reality of our lives, owe it to ourselves to give careful attention to our manner of speaking, to give the words we use about ourselves weight, gravity, body, substance, heat, heart.

That's the end of my sermon against the devil and all his words. It's true that you've got to *make your own kind of music, sing your own special song*. It's not easy, finding the right words – but terribly important that we try. A song says, "*It's only words, but words are all I have to steal your heart away*." When we feel caught *between the devil and the deep blue sea*, at a loss for words, *try to remember*: there's no shortage of lyrics. Just about every heartache has its lament and every joy has a great backbeat. So even though it means muddling through in confusion to find the best words, and *smoke gets in your eyes*, remember too that your *heart has a mind of its own*, and *don't let the moon break your heart*. And when you want to say the most important words of all, just *put your sweet lips a little closer to the phone* and say, "*You can eat crackers in my bed anytime.*"

Notes

1. James Hillman, *Re-Visioning Psychology*, New York: Harper & Row, 1975, p. x.
2. George Orwell, *1984*, New York: New American Library, 1981, paperback edition, p. 253 (appendix).
3. Ibid., p. 254.

Chapter 3

Women and the land

Imagination and reality

While our worries about "subversion" are usually political, there are other ways in which subversion takes its psychological toll. Subversion is an important way of psychologically studying phenomena, but it is also something that happens to us: if we do not turn a subversive eye on our own culture, the culture will subvert us, turn us under and keep us unconscious about the most basic kinds of knowledge which should be our birthright. Those things about which we ought to be most conscious and to which we ought to be most naturally and organically connected, are just those things from which cultural attitudes, prejudice, and history cut us off and keep us *un*conscious. I imagine as a psychological ideal an adaptation in which we all have a sharper, instinctive sense of our own physical bodies, sensitivity to wild animals and their habitats as if we were co-relatives and co-habitants, responsiveness to climate, and an appreciation of the land itself.

Urban dwellers are perhaps most vulnerable to being subverted in these ways. Fitness programs, ski weekends, camping trips, and vacation tours through Disneyworld are fun but not radical attempts to see through to how subverted we've been and how deeply disconnected we are from the very ground on which we walk. It is no wonder that in our culture we do not usually and respectfully take off our shoes and call our ground "holy."

Since subversion is itself an "underground" activity, the fact and idea of "ground" is worth examining as an experience from the perspective of the soul, and especially from a soul in exile from its ancestral land. One of the most fruitful ways to cultivate one's psychic ground is to recollect and remember, so I am casting this essay in the form of a reminiscence.

I used to think "land" was just "dirt." I used to think "land" was just "the ground," not hearing any metaphorical resonance in that, no deeper sense of ground, being grounded, standing one's ground. Ground was just something you were not supposed to be under, because if you were it meant you were a political threat or you were dead. "Ground" is not a very romantic word; it sometimes carries a suggestion of defeat, or exhaustion: being ground down, the daily grind, knocked flat on the ground, having the ground give way under you.

But "land" is nearly always a poetic, romantic word, a word that often appears with other pleasant, poetic words: the land of the free, a land of milk and honey, a green and verdant land, home land, promised land. We don't want to give ground, but we ask to be given land, lots of land.

Since I am only one part rural and three parts urban, my images of land have been somewhat romanticized in the absence of a solid, grounded relationship to land. I didn't even make mud pies when I was a kid. I was born in Brooklyn, New York, in 1942, and I remember only concrete until I was eight years old. I walked to school and back every day, but what I saw was cement and iron fences, cement and brownstone houses, cement and asphalt roads, cement sidewalks and cement subways.

Then, in 1951, my parents bought a house and we moved to Long Island. We were first-generation suburbanites, living just a few miles from famous Levittown in a large subdivision of houses still under construction when we moved in. There was dirt everywhere, of which my mother complained – we were not to track it in, the dust was impossible, there was gravel in the new wall-to-wall carpeting in the living room, when would they finish paving the roads already? My father set about immediately covering the exposed ground outside around the house, as if its nakedness was a silent criticism of his husbandry. The dirt of the plot was graded and topsoiled and graded again, rocks handpicked out. We had a corner plot, and my father put little wooden stakes all around the plot, with string and little white rag strips hanging from it. This was to keep human feet off the new grass that had been planted. Narrow cement walks were laid to front and side doors.

None of us ever thought of this little corner plot as our *land*, our ground. We thought of it, and spoke of it, as "the house" and "the lawn." We lived in the house, and the lawn lived around us. For me growing up there and imagining my future, the "plot" came to mean a fearful conspiracy to trap me into suburban life.

But there was a rural part of me too. My grandfather owned about two hundred acres in what was then a secluded, forested, mountainous region of central New Jersey. I spent every summer there every year for seventeen years, although I only remember the years beginning at age six when I started riding horseback. When I was there, in the late 1940s and through the '50s, there were few paved roads, houses were miles apart and most of them farms. Within just half a mile of my grandfather's house you could be lost in the forest, and my cousin and I often were. But still, all that acreage in New Jersey, all that wildness, and freedom of movement, and sense of expansion – the exhilaration of unlimited possibilities because no one seemed to *own* all that land – with all this, there was no conception in my family of "the land," not even "our land." It was "property." Buildable, developable, taxable, rentable, appreciable, property.

Brooklyn cement, Long Island plot, New Jersey property. These are not nourishing, romantic, poetic images. They are images of small, pinched living, life measured in square feet and acres, quality of life measured in the absence of weeds in the lawn.

My family was not psychologically able to put down roots that penetrated through the concrete; they were not able to develop and transmit to me a sense of rootedness and being grounded, even though they owned some land and the titles to it were legally secure. I do not think this was because they were just greedy materialists or because they were shallow and incapable of psychological depth. I think it was more that the collective prevailing attitude of *controlling* the land took as its sacrifice a sense of *working with* the land. And secondly, I think it was because my family are all Jews, which historically has meant (among other things) a condition of exile and forced wandering. Our attitude toward land was conditioned more by our Jewish history of migrancy than by the fact of actual ownership in modern America. After centuries of displacements, it is hard to settle down in just a generation or two.

One's ethnic history determines the basic formations of one's psyche, its geological configurations, if you will. But however modern and removed from the past we may think we are, psyche remembers the great mythic images of land: virginal and unspoiled, lush, like a woman's body: wild in dance, soft, curved, vulnerable to plows, receptive to seed, and capable of erupting with furious volcanic passion in fire that can melt rock and destroy what men have built. The somewhat romantic notion some of us have about "returning to nature" or "communing with nature" or "getting back to nature" is a recognition that we are separated from nature. It is a double metaphor expressing the psychological reality that we have lost, or been robbed of, the sense of the natural world and the sensuality of our natural bodies. The separation of a woman from her "land" is an interior separation of a woman from her own body: both land and body have been appropriated to an unnatural degree primarily for male purposes, and both have become property, with all that implies: territorial rights, boundaries, no trespassing signs, control of production and repro-duction. After all, a husband is both a keeper of the land and a husband.

I know in myself and in my body the volcanic rage that accompanies enforced exile from the land. I know this in my blood as a Jew, having witnessed in my own lifetime both Holocaust and recreation of homeland in Israel. And I know the rage that is the proper and inevitable response of the dispossessed, and the rage that comes when my rage is dismissed as paranoia or personal psychopathology. It may be more than just a quirky personal association on my part to note that the gas chambers of the death camps were built of cement, and so are our so-called freeways and other reinforced concrete bunkers in our minds.

My own roots have to pass through the concrete of Brooklyn pavement if I am to be grounded at all. I was born separated from the earth by femaleness, by Jewishness, and by concrete, and at a time when my people were being returned to the earth in ashes by the millions. And I believe that as women we share a collective psychic ground, which has also been covered over by concrete so that we cannot see it, and often we cannot even feel it.

The ancient image of women in relation to land is that women *are* land; but the reality of our lives is that this image has been both degraded and overly romanticized; and also concretized, made literal – so that we do not truly own our bodies any more than we truly own the land. Most of the land now belongs to giant agri-businesses, or oil companies, or banks, or is owned by the State, to be controlled, managed, zoned, preserved or reserved, as if the living earth – woman – doesn't know how or can't be trusted to take care of herself, and is incapable of *self*-possession.

We have to go *under* ground to find out who we are as women; self-knowledge requires that we be psychologically subversive. We are *not* just potentially fertile females waiting to be plowed and fulfilled – this is a male idea of woman-as-land. Under the ground, under this male image of land, there is another reality, there are other images of women's bodily and psychological reality. "Underground" is not just mysteriously dark and sexually damp, it is also brightly lit with hot fires at the earth's core that keeps earth alive with body heat; there are vast expanses of thick continental shelves, moving in shifts of slow, sure power to change the face of the world. Underground there are coral beds, artesian wells, oil deposits, icebergs and fossils. All of which may have many meanings attached to them – coral beds of deceptive beauty and natural formations, wells of clean renewal, unlimited wealth of valuable deposits as yet unclaimed by women, icebergs of implacable purpose and hatred where necessary, and fossils – the memory of our foremothers, whose bodies bore us and whose images are still imprinted in our souls as in rock, even though long sealed and buried under layers of soil and oppression.

A double reclamation of land by women has to take place. Literally, we must reclaim the land as earth because she is our mother and without her to nourish and provide foundation, we all perish, and other species with us. The second reclamation is psychological: we need to reclaim the land and give it dignity in the form of our own bodies. We need to re-image land from a female imagination. This is a compelling necessity for women, whose bodies have been imaged in metaphors of earth and ground and land and treated patriarchally and patronizingly the same way: owned, rented, harvested, exploited, exhausted, platted, plotted, parceled out, covered over, landscaped, plowed, stripped, furrowed, seeded, fenced, staked out, claimed, bought and sold. A friend of mine says that "every woman is a colonized nation." She is right. No woman is in actuality sovereign. And even though every woman has a rightful claim to her own body, historically it too often has been physically hazardous, psychologically crippling, spiritually exhausting, and economically suicidal for her to exercise that claim, when it has been possible for her to do so at all.

One of the ways this reclamation takes place is through memory. This is one of the ways historians and storytellers keep us alive. Another way of reclaiming our land, our bodies, is through poetry, a sensual body and language of images that speaks the way the land itself speaks: in pulsing rhythms, currents of rivers, falls of water, aspirations and hopes of mountain peaks, desolate beauty of deserts, and the horror and ugliness of land fills and toxic waste dumps. Women who are filmmakers, novelists, musicians, sculptors – all those engaged in the creative arts – are at work reclaiming our creative ground: their generative work is regeneration for all of us, for we need their art, their produce, to live. Theirs is the fruit of the earth.

And another way of reclaiming the land is the concrete working of it. This is very different than working concrete over it, which was the only way I knew as a child. Working it, tending it, turning it over, planting it, worrying about the weather and insects and diseases, dreaming it, sifting through it, feeding it, watering it, dancing on it, clearing it, leaving parts of it alone for a while – all of these are the concrete labors of land workers, and they are also the concrete labors of women caring for their physical and psychic bodies. One's psyche is a farm and must be worked the same way. One's physical body needs all this farming and one's soul needs all this cultivating. Like the land, we are seasonal, we have psychological cycles and metabolic rhythms. And sometimes the process of reclamation, of restoring ourselves, requires a seventh day of complete rest.

I want to end with part of a poem by Gertrud Kolmar, a German Jewish poet whose forty-eight-year-old body was burned at Auschwitz sometime in 1943. She is one of our foremothers, whose ashes are now part of our earth. The poem is called "Woman Undiscovered."

> I too am a continent.
> I have unexplored mountains, bushlands
>   impenetrable and lost,
> Bays, stream-deltas, salt-licking tongues
>   of coast,
> Caves where giant crawling beasts gleam
>   dusky green,
> And inland seas where lemon-yellow
>   jellyfish are seen.
>
> No rains have washed my budded breasts,
> No springs burst forth from them: these
>   gardens are remote from all the rest.
> And no adventurer has claimed my desert
>   valley's golden sands,
> Or crossed the virgin snows atop my
>   highest barren lands. . . .
>
> Above me, often skies are black with stars
>   or bright with thunder storms;
> Inside me flicker lobed and jagged craters
>   filled with violent glowing forms;
> But an ice-pure fountain I have as well,
>   and the flower that drinks there quietly:
> I am a continent that one day soon will
>   sink without a sound into the sea.[1]

Notes

1. Gertrud Kolmar, *Dark Soliloquy: The Selected Poems of Gertrud Kolmar*, (translated from the German by Henry A. Smith), New York: The Seabury Press, 1975, pp. 59, 61.

Chapter 4

"Taking The Dark With Open Eyes"

Hidden dimensions of a psychology of abortion

If I can take the dark with open eyes
And call it seasonal, not harsh or strange . . .
And, treelike, stand unmoved before the
    change,
Lose what I lose to keep what I can keep,
The strong root still alive under the snow,
Love will endure – if I can let you go.[1]
      (May Sarton, "Taking the Dark With
        Open Eyes," from *Autumn Sonnets*)

Say the word *abortion* in America and you light a fuse that detonates a powerful emotional and sometimes physically violent debate. To some abortion is a blasphemy, to others a symbol of the most fundamental right to govern decisions of an individual's most intimate life. The way we Americans respond to abortion – the word, the concept, the fact – trumpets the existence of a fierce collective psychological complex. A complex of this depth and magnitude is a more-than-the-sum total of all our individual thoughts and feelings about abortion.

The *word* is loaded. The *idea* of abortion is deeply meshed with our ideas about power, control, and being "civilized." And though the capacity to regulate the timing and number of offspring is not unique to humans, when a female of our species willfully and consciously terminates a pregnancy, it is impossible for us to regard it as nothing more than a biological response to environmental conditions. Such a termination always involves an intricate set of emotions, both on the part of the pregnant woman and of the culture in which she lives.

Most psychological and counseling professionals have been occupied with the ego-level decision-making process of a woman considering abortion, and with the aftermath of such a decision. The inevitability of serious depression as a consequence of aborting a pregnancy is generally assumed – a prejudice held over from the last century when it was irrefutable dogma that a woman can only be fulfilled and happy when she has children, and must become depressed and miserable if she does not. In 1886, the great Austrian psychiatrist Richard von Krafft-Ebing wrote that a woman will not suffer with dread the coming of menopause and the end of her productive life if "her sexual career has been successful, and loving children gladden the maternal heart."[2] Even today we do not hear much about those women who consider abortion but decide, or are required, to carry to term and *then* become depressed.

The legal choice used to be: get pregnant and have children, or, get pregnant and have children. This "choice" was also a social requirement for women. In the public mind there was no *moral* choice, since no one, or no one who mattered, considered that the bearing of a child might in some circumstances be immoral. For married women, an abortion could never be a moral choice, for it contradicted the very purpose of marriage, and deprived her husband of *his* offspring. Even for unmarried women, the crushing shame attached to an out-of-wedlock birth was light compared to the moral horror of a woman terminating the tiny life in her own body.

In the heated public discourse about abortion, the deeper psychological point of view has been conspicuously absent. Psyche's perspective, which has to do with possible *meanings* of a woman's termination of pregnancy, is the hidden dimension of the complex that has been obscured by politics, religion, sociology, medicine, and the advertising industry. By positioning abortion in the religious sphere of morality or the political realm of social policy, everyone has a position on the matter. But psyche is not a position; it is that image-making faculty in us through which we perceive and understand our reality. To "understand" abortion, then, is to stand under it and try to see what fundamental psychological image, or idea, or necessity, is expressing itself in the social arenas of debate.

The psychological place to begin talking about abortion is in the psyche's own language, the language of image. Experience is differentiated through language, and each arena of debate about abortion has its own vocabulary. *Politics* uses the language of rights: who has the right to make decisions about other people's rights. *Law* talks about abortion in terms such as jurisdiction, criminality, liability, constitutional rights to privacy. *Religion* uses the language of morality: wrong or right, bad or good, sinful or acceptable in the sight of God. *Medicine* uses the language of biology: fetal viability, genetic dispositions, congenital defects, risk to the mother's physical health. And so on.

The human psyche has its own language, which is less verbal than imagistic; it does not speak in concepts and categories, but in *images* that personify ideas and that animate us with their inherent emotional qualities. The *psychological* question of abortion is, "What images arise in the psyche of a woman who voluntarily aborts a pregnancy?" One way to find these images is to ask metaphorically, "Who does a woman who aborts a pregnancy look like?"

Recognizing Artemis

A woman who aborts a fetus looks like a woman able to live in the realm of the goddess known to the ancient Greeks as Artemis, to the Romans as Diana, to Candomble believers in Brazil as Oxum, and in other cultures by other names. The pattern of consciousness or attitude personified by this goddess is the backdrop against which a particular understanding of pregnancy, childbirth, and abortion is formed. In an individual woman (whose psychological disposition inclines her to that way of understanding), "Artemis" functions as that deep, remote pattern of energy, that particular perspective of the world that evaluates experience in terms of female intactness and bodily integrity. In the Artemisian world, anyone who threatens a woman's sense of completeness, psychological and physical, is deemed inimical to her life and honor. The consciousness personified by Artemis is connected with virginity in the psychological, not sexual, sense; that is, a woman who is complete unto herself.[3] But, strikingly, this Artemisian perspective is also concerned with wild, pristine nature and care of the young and most vulnerable creatures.

I suggest that the problem our culture has with Artemis is the problem we have with abortion. By looking into the nature of this divinity, we find a way to look differently at the experience of abortion, a perspective from the mythic depth of the soul, or psyche.

In a world that is sophisticated, domesticated, and largely urban, Artemis is not welcome. She is not interested in intimacy and inter-personal relationships, nor in community. She does not know the meaning of "co-dependent" and has no "issues" to "work on." She would not be caught within fifty miles of any kind of support group. She reveals herself in those with a certain kind of wild and independent spirit. Queen Elizabeth I once said, "I will have but one mistress in this house and no master," and thus gave voice to living Artemis.

Artemis is known as the strange, distant one, the remote one, unapproachable, the one who comes from far away. When she does manifest in our lives, there is often an ominous sense of mystery because she is so foreign to our "civilized" ways of being. She who loves the freedom of solitude and wilderness would go mad in a world like ours, full of arbitrary moral prohibitions and scientific manipulations that seek to override the *natural* course of life and death. In her realm, death and life are merely two aspects of the same thing – the cycle of nature. Christine Downing says, "Artemis *is herself* the wilderness, the wild and untamed, and not simply its mistress."[4]

Downing writes of Artemis as the one who is fearlessly self-sufficient, and when she manifests in a woman's consciousness, that woman is serious, committed, utterly uncompromising. Artemis brings to consciousness the necessity of choosing *oneself*, a choice that confronts every adolescent entering adulthood. But it is a choice especially difficult for girls, who are still taught from birth to choose someone else – a husband, for example. Artemis is the personification of a woman's essential, core integrity of which she becomes conscious by choosing herself. And though our culture professes to value these qualities of self-sufficiency, integrity, and incorruptibility, they are often still judged as liabilities in women: the Artemisian woman is thought to be aloof and cold, hard and ruthless. Our culture fears and discredits Artemis when she makes her epiphany in a woman.

Artemis unites seemingly incompatible values. She personifies that awful and awesome solitude where a woman is utterly alone and inaccessible, yet she attracts to herself companions who are like her. As hunter, her kills are quick and clean, because while death is natural, the unnecessary suffering of wounds caused by the hunter is not. And though her arrows never miss their aim when they pierce our consciousness with the demand for adult independence, she herself becomes the hunted one who flees the voyeuristic encroachment of those who seek to possess or destroy her. As constrained nature, she will strike ruthlessly and suddenly against any who violate her. But she is also the great maternal protector of all young, wild, and vulnerable creatures: animals and children.

I suspect that abortion was a more straightforward thing in the old times now gone from living memory, that time when women honored Artemis by living congruently with their instincts – including self-preservation. That time may have no documented history, but lives in us through mythic tradition, just as Artemis the Goddess is not a historical figure but a mythic, psychic pattern of behavior. In that mythic time women kept their own counsel, their own wisdom, about matters that did not pertain to men, such as moon and blood cycles, birthing, and the particularly female kind of sexual pleasure that men could not imagine.

Women had abortions in those times for most of the same reasons women have them now, because they could not or would not ensure the child what it needed for viability: they could not get enough food for one, or for one more; they were sick; if they got sick they could not work; they were poor; they were too young, or too old; they were afraid the child would be born deformed or under a curse, that it would not live long or well; the father was unknown, or unwilling, or untrustworthy, or too poor, or dead; they were afraid of not knowing what to do; and they were afraid of dying.

In those ancient times, law and religious sanctions and economics and the male need for proprietorship were no less forceful than they are now; in some external ways they were even more so. But women had not yet completely absorbed those man-made laws and theologies and medical dictums; they had not yet so totally *intro*jected, or accepted within themselves, the values of the male world that they were cut off from the original source of their own female physical wisdom, as many women are today. They had not yet lost contact with the deepest female knowings of when it is time for life, and when it is time for death.

All female animals know this. In nature, the reproductive cycle of most female animals changes when food supplies become scarce or environmental conditions become too harsh to support young life. Female birds and mammals do not then ovulate, in effect preventing untimely reproduction in spite of the males' blind urge to mate. Once, human females could do this too, by ingesting certain herbs and roots to induce miscarriage. They acted from the same natural instinct, that instinctive response that serves Artemis and is preserved by her.

Artemis was also known as the midwife, invoked in ancient times by women in labor because her own mother Leto bore her with no pain. As soon as Artemis entered the world, the Fates appointed her to midwife the birth of her twin brother Apollo. And so she is the goddess who is present at every birth and every death, midwifing the transitions, the death of the old and the birth of the new. In particular, she presides over the passage of young girls into womanhood – which is both a birth and a death – because she embodies and personifies the most elemental natural rhythms and transitions of the life cycle. Indeed, she is present whenever a woman of any age prepares to undergo yet another step in maturation. And in the way of the virgin, Artemis remains unmerged with and separate from those young girls and women who are her chosen companions; her sexuality is for pleasure and is in the service of neither reproduction nor relationship.

The Bible says that to everything there is a season: a time to be born, and a time to die. But the times of being born and dying are, for us humans, times of profound mystery. Abortion is a death that a woman experiences in her own living body, usually by her own will; often it happens privately, almost invisibly. The Latin root of the word "abortion" means, literally, "to disappear." In our culture the public debate and rhetoric and positions are open and loud and everywhere visible in our national life, but the *experience* of the woman who aborts her pregnancy too often disappears. Not only her pregnancy is aborted, but her experience of its termination is aborted and disappears as well. We have to keep in mind that the Latin root of the word "experience" means "to lead out of peril." Here again Artemis is to be invoked, for as with all other birthings, she presides over perilous transitions in a woman's life as she midwifes meaning in the psyche.

A few years ago, at a large public debate at Columbia University, Illinois Congressman Henry Hyde – a white-haired, white-skinned, well-groomed sixty-something gentleman – declared that he opposed *all* abortion except to save the mother's life. When asked why he would not make an exception even for a conception resulting from rape or incest, he replied that there should not be a secondary victim of the crime; the unborn child's "claim [to life] is equal [to the mother's] – a life for a life." I think it is precisely this inability – or refusal – to differentiate between mature life and nascent life, between conscious, responsible, independent life and unconscious, reflexive, dependent life, that constellates Artemis and draws her to the scene. It is Artemis in me who wants to ask Henry Hyde if he considers his life equal to that of a ten-week-old fetus.

Artemis and men

One of the reasons Artemis is feared in our sex-obsessed culture is because it is forbidden to men to look upon the beautiful Artemis naked, to try to penetrate her mystery, to trespass in her private, interior realms. Artemis does not suffer voyeurs. When he trespasses into questions that belong in the domain of Artemis, the civilized Congressman Henry Hyde, for example, is potentially a modern Actaeon, the legendary hunter who gazed upon Artemis bathing nude. The goddess punished him for this trespass by turning him into a stag so that his own dogs tore him to pieces. She who midwifes life and also brings death will have her revenge if her domain is violated by intruders. She is as capable of killing in vengeance as she is of killing in mercy, and the arrows of Artemis, whose name means "She Who Slays," always find their mark.

There is a profound mystery in abortion, a mystery of female power, which is still something of a contradiction in terms. It is a mystery of death, which we fear and deny; a mystery of life, which does not yield its secret meanings easily; and a mystery of sacrifice, which we have so much trouble understanding because it has to do with love, about which we know so little.

That a woman may bring the recreation of her own flesh and blood to death before its birth is, in the deepest sense, a sacrifice. It is one of the great mysteries. Perhaps the reason we become so inflamed about abortion in our time is not because it is so "controversial," not because it is so "political," and not because it is inherently "moral" or "immoral." We become inflamed because it is a mystery that we do not understand, do not want to face. It is terrifying. It is a mystery like Artemis, protector of the young and yet, "She Who Slays."

At the heart of this mystery is the power of women over life and death. Men may have a harder and more fearful time with this mystery because the primal power of life belongs to woman, and thus most certainly she wields the power of death. That primal power of life is a biological impossibility for a man. He can never be a true matrix of that mystery. It is possible that at least part of what fuels "patriarchy" – the rule of the fathers – is a belligerent, resentful, compensatory response to the fathers' fearful and precarious position.

In a culture which has no significant female deity and is ruled by a male god, this life-and-death power has been appropriated to *him*. The giving of life through women still retains a sense of *mystery*, but the taking of life by women is a *sacrilege*. When this power is exercised in abortion, legally or not, it contradicts our most cherished and exalted image of the male-defined meaning of "mother."

Artemis and Mother

If we expect "Mother" to be the source of abundant nourishment, the model of infinite sacrifice for the child's well-being, and the fount of limitless love and devotion – all of which we *do* expect – then the mother who voluntarily aborts her child utterly destroys those expectations, destroys paradise. She is a monster, an abomination, an unnatural woman. This is simply not how we expect women to behave. However, our expectations of men betray an appalling double standard and hidden contempt: though we feel shock and grief and rage when *they* act like monsters, we secretly expect a dark side and are not really surprised when it appears.

A woman who aborts presents us with an image of the mother who has the godlike power to destroy each of us, who ejects us coldly from the womb, that safe, life-giving haven we think nature intended it to be.

Such a godlike woman becomes a person of ultimate consequence. It is a profoundly tragic irony that a woman's sacrifice of her fetus is counted of far greater import in our country than the fact that this same woman may be raped, beaten, or murdered in less time than it takes for me to write this sentence. It is equally chilling to consider how many are raped, beaten, and murdered *because* they have this fearsome godlike power.

For centuries, the rhetoric of abortion, and particularly religious rhetoric, has condemned women who abort for selfishness, unnatural selfishness, sinful selfishness, making it clear that the real crime a woman commits is not the termination of her pregnancy, but the prerogative of valuing her own life, her own viability, over another's. Again, this flies in the face of everything we expect a mother to be.

We can see just how deep this cultural expectation is by the prevalence, for example, of Jewish mother jokes: the stereotypical Jewish mother is completely antithetical to Artemisian consciousness. When she prepares the family meal, the "Jewish mother" is expected to eat only a few ounces so that there will be that much more food for her children – and still she worries that they will starve. Jewish mother jokes are funny because they exaggeratedly express a truism about how devoted mothers are to children. But the humor also provides insulation from the deeper and secret sense of fear that at any moment, that same mother may instead turn on her children and eat them.

The depth of our expectation of the mother as supremely self-sacrificing is embodied in the image of the Virgin Mary, a central image of "femininity" in our culture. In her, virginity is exalted because it makes *divine* motherhood possible; in her, motherhood is the essence of femaleness that makes biology into destiny. Every woman who aborts a pregnancy appears, in the collective view, as a polar opposite of the Virgin. She is not all-embracing, life-giving mother; she is selfish, very selfish, totally selfish. She does not acquiesce, and this is the second worst crime women can commit. The *first* worst crime is to imagine that she actually, not rhetorically, has power over her body – that she has the power and *authority* to decide whether to bear or not to bear a child conceived in her womb – even a divine one.

Artemis and the American child

And here is another compelling reason why abortion has become a painful collective complex for us. We have such trouble with Artemisian consciousness, and women who at times act from that consciousness, because our culture is held in thrall by the archetypal image of the Child.

As long as this archetype dominates and is the supreme value of one's inner life, there is little hope of resolving the abortion complex. For if the child is the primary divine figure, then to kill it is not only infanticide, but *deicide*; and if it demands so much attention as one's *central* inner figure, then to abort it is to commit a kind of suicide.

On a less profound level, cultures of longer histories than ours accuse Americans of youth worship and of indulging in the longest collective adolescence on the planet. While we elevate the child's longings for comfort, safety, and feeling good as our highest values, the rest of the world regards us as irresponsible, undisciplined, and self-absorbed.

Consider the astounding proliferation of "help books" on the theme of "the inner child" or "the child within." One promotion in a psychology catalog gives assurance that by reading the advertised book, you will learn that if you feel anxious, depressed, or angry "*without reason*," then you have probably "identified with a childhood experience." (As if there were no reason to feel this way as an adult in the present world!) Further, the author will teach you to find your inner child, whereupon you will "learn to love, nurture and respect this little person."

But Artemisian consciousness resists this infantilizing of the adult psyche. My child has not read Shakespeare, has not been entranced by Donatello's sculpture, been moved by the language of Toni Morrison, or been delighted by a Mozart opera. Even though it is rather adorable and wonderfully engaging and playful, my "inner child" remains a child, uneducated and illiterate, and while my attitude toward it is important, it is not the *only* imaginal figure that is important, and not the *most* important most of the time.

Sacrifice

It is true that in the world of Artemis, that world of wild nature, there is no place where death may not enter. There is no law that says it is illegal, immoral, unnecessary, or unjust that young things die: that fawns may not freeze in the cold or that rabbits may not be eaten by wolves, or that lionesses may not kill some of their young if food is insufficient. This "natural law" is much older than man's theistic inventions and "civilized" constructs, and this is probably why Artemisian consciousness appears to us as cold, cruel, and psychopathic. Such deaths, we think, are avoidable, or with modern technology, at least postponable. But a woman who is moved by Artemis to abort her pregnancy presents us with a different understanding of death: death as sacrifice, death of a living part of oneself as a sacrificial offering.

Since we moderns have lost nearly all contact with Artemis, with that way of understanding life and death and the inviolability of women's bodies, we view abortion as an avoidable, unnatural, wasteful death rather than a sacrificial death in which there is meaning. Our culture says the woman who chooses to abort becomes like Artemis, remote, cruel, heartless, a woman far away from conventional morality and social norms. Or else she is young and immature, sexually wild, promiscuous, and irresponsible – by either of which we mean a woman who contradicts all the cultural expectations of what a "mother" should be.

Because this condemnatory collective judgment is very old, and reinforced through daily repetition in our newspapers and courts and clinics and churches, the woman who terminates her pregnancy may have a rough time returning to the integrity of her interior self and appreciating *herself* as sacrifice to Artemis. A woman who has had an abortion by choice has made a sacrifice; she has also become a sacrifice. For a woman is not separate from her pregnancy, any more than Artemis is separate from her virginity. A pregnant woman is not merely a carrier, a walking womb, any more than a man is merely a life support system for a penis. When a woman aborts, something of her life, her living body, has been killed. She also has had to offer up on the altar of Artemis something of her old way of being, in whatever way that mattered: she has passed through sorrow and loss; she has given up one of her futures. No longer is she innocent, naïve, all-nurturing. No matter what her age, she is no longer truly young and inexperienced; she may even sacrifice love and respect in a relationship or marriage. Sometimes she may sacrifice her own deep desire to bear the child because her mate is unable or unwilling to help provide the love and sustenance that is a child's birthright.[5]

Whatever it means to her, having an abortion changes a woman. In the best of circumstances she discovers her capacity to sacrifice, and sacrifice is one way in which we measure the capacity to love. Perhaps it is the consciousness of abortion as a meaningful sacrifice that takes it out of the realm of personal selfishness and puts it into the context of some deeper necessity, some deeper purpose she must serve. For where there is meaning, there is a divine presence.

There are a thousand reasons why women decide to abort a pregnancy; but in every instance, a sacrifice is being made, consciously or unconsciously. And it is only the individual woman who can say, if she knows, what that sacrifice is and what it means to her to offer it.[6] Accusations of murder, selfishness, promiscuity, and irresponsibility are all ways of *avoiding* the meaning of the woman's experience, ways of refusing to regard her decision to abort as something more than self-indulgence, something less than criminal, something other than bad judgment. Such accusations are, at bottom, judgments that her sacrifice is unworthy and so is she; and I for one cannot understand how a woman can be condemned for *her* sacrifice, while we hold as a spiritual ideal of obedience the old patriarch Abraham with a knife to his thirteen-year-old son's throat.

When Artemis comes to a pregnant woman, she comes either as midwife or as "She Who Slays," she who requires sacrifice for the sake of the mother's integrity, physical well-being, or for the sake of any young for whom there may be fates worse than death. The concern of Artemis as midwife is not based on a morality requiring that life be preserved in all circumstances at all cost; it is not a morality that glorifies Life as a capital L, transcendent abstraction without regard to the quality of individual life. And it is not a morality that conceptually extracts individual life from the collective context and environment that must support it.

Artemisian morality knows, as every mother knows, that nothing is more cruel than the suffering of children. For a woman to bear a child she does not want is a violence perpetrated upon the child. The bond of love and desire which should provide the psychological environment in which the child may thrive is broken or contaminated even before birth, because the mother is not right with herself and cannot willingly provide psychological nourishment to the child. The child comes into the world already wounded.

The conscious decision of a woman to abort a pregnancy involves, to some degree, recognition of a collective good. And in this, too, Artemis is present in the woman's concern to protect and spare the young and vulnerable from unnecessary suffering. From the perspective of Artemis, it is a violation of nature, an affront to the goddess whose special province is the care of small and helpless creatures, to bring children into a family or community or country or world in which they will not be given all those things that make for true viability. In this sense, viability is a psychological concern, not a medical definition. From the Artemisian perspective, the debate is not about when the embryo becomes a fetus becomes a baby becomes viable, but rather the circumstances under which it is good for the child to be midwifed from the womb to the world.

Until the advent of modern fertility medicine, the word *viability* meant something much larger than whether a fertilized egg with no developed neurological system was "viable," or whether a six-month-old fetus was physically viable outside the womb. Viability means, literally, the ability to live, and "life" is always something more for human beings than mere existence, more than the lung capacity to inhale and exhale, more than the brain's ability to produce a blip on a monitoring screen. A viable child is one who is welcomed into a larger body than its mother's, who comes well into a community able and willing to receive it and sustain it for years. In the absence of provision for the child's food, housing, medicine, future education, the promise of meaningful work, and/or the absence of love, desire, and responsible maturity in the procreators for their child, the maternal concern for the well-being of the child may consider abortion the best course. In such an instance it is, again, usually Artemis, the unseen, ancient, intact wisdom of nature, that moves a woman to act on behalf of her child by aborting it. She makes the decision in maternal consideration of the child's viability – the same consideration that moves Artemis to kill a wounded fawn rather than force it to live crippled and defenseless.

As with any deep, painful complex in an individual psyche, there is little likelihood that our national abortion complex will be thoroughly untangled, let alone finally resolved. As long as women get pregnant, some pregnancies will be aborted – by accident, by coercion, or by choice. Neither legislation, nor religion, nor politics, nor social disapproval will prevent women from seeking abortion. None of these has ever done so historically, does not now, and will not in the future. Rather than look for solutions to the so-called *problem* of abortion, we might productively look for meanings in the experience of abortion. We become trespassers in the domain of the great goddess Artemis and her mysteries of primal life and death when *our* laws are forcibly imposed on her. Like Actaeon the hunter, if we try arrogantly to penetrate her mystery, we risk having our collective national body torn to pieces.

So long as human beings attach meaning and dignity to individual life, there will be sacrifices made to preserve meaning and dignity. Our first responsibility is not to condemn, outlaw, and bemoan abortion, but to ensure that such sacrifices are not made in vain.

The story I close with here was given to me by my friend, Clarissa Pinkola-Estes. It is a very old story that comes from the psyche's mythic ground, and therefore is a true, but not literal, story. The people of Mexico know of the goddess named Tsati, who always appears carrying a great bowl. Her bowl is both breast and grave. When turned one way, the bowl is a great breast pouring out life-sustaining milk; when turned another way, the bowl is a coffin. The goddess Tsati comes when you are dying; gently she sets you in her great bowl and begins to swirl you around. And as the bowl swirls around and around, you become smaller and smaller, and younger and younger, and then Tsati pours you from her bowl into a woman's womb so that you may again come forth into life.

Notes

1. May Sarton, from *Autumn Sonnets*, in Serena Sue Hilsinger and Lois Brynes (eds) *Selected Poems of May Sarton*, New York: W. W. Norton & Co. Inc., p. 51.
2. Richard von Krafft-Ebing, *Psychopathia Sexualis*, translated by Franklin S. Klaf from twelfth German edition, New York: Stein and Day, 1965, p. 8.
3. For a psychology of Artemis and her style of consciousness, the following works are suggested: Nor Hall, *The Moon and the Virgin*, New York: Harper & Row, 1980; Christine Downing, *Goddess*, New York: Crossroad Publishing Co., 1984; Ginette Paris, *Pagan Meditations*, Dallas: Spring Publications, 1986. Some sources for ancient stories about Artemis are: Edward Tripp, *The Meridian Handbook of Classical Mythology*, New York: Penguin Books, 1970; Karl Kerenyi, *The Gods of the Greeks*, London: Thames and Hudson, 1951; and Michael Grant and John Hazel, *Who's Who in Classical Mythology*, London: Weidenfeld and Nicolson, 1973.
4. Christine Downing, *Goddess*, New York: Crossroad Publishing Co., 1984, p. 165.
5. For a full and rich discussion of Artemis, with particular attention to childbirth and abortion, see Ginette Paris, "Artemis," Chapter 8 in *Pagan Meditations*, Dallas: Spring Publications, Inc., 1986.
6. Some women do abort a fetus out of selfishness, and, certainly, not every woman who aborts her pregnancy does so consciously. So it is questionable to what degree a psychology of Artemisian sacrifice applies in such a case. A genuine sacrifice must be a conscious act, or it is not a true sacrifice. Many women, and especially girls still in their adolescence, abort out of fear, in panic, and act thoughtlessly of consequences. But at some point in her life a woman must come to terms with the fact of the abortion. Whenever that happens, the meaning of the experience can be made conscious, and it may happen at that time, even much later in life, that the sacrificial aspect of the abortion becomes part of its meaning.

Chapter 5

False memories, true memory, and maybes

> The self-absorption that seems to be the impetus and embarrassment of autobiography turns into (or perhaps always was) a hunger for the world. Actually, it begins as hunger for *a* world, one gone or lost, effaced by time or a more sudden brutality. But in the act of remembering, the personal environment expands, resonates beyond itself, beyond its "subject," into the endless and tragic recollection that is history.
>
> (Patricia Hampl, "Memory and Imagination"[1])

Once upon a time, a long time ago, far away, the great Goddess Mnemosyne, whose name means *memory* in our language, lived in the high mountains of Greece, and was greatly honored through her nine daughters, the Muses. Zeus was their father, he who discerns the truth in all matters, and so the Muses inherit from him their truthfulness, expressing it in many forms. For everyone knew that the most necessary "truth" of the human soul was found not in science laboratories and databanks, but in poetry and song, in fine art and drama, and chorales: all those modes that give voice to what humans remember and envision.

Mnemosyne keeps all remembrance, all history, alive within herself. Her beautiful daughters, the Muses, serve and honor her by rendering her substance, history, into art, so that what lives in memory is made into images that speak truthfully of the human condition. The Muses take individual memories, and the collective memories of a people, and turn them into the chorale of history, so that we know who we are and where we come from.

But the Goddess of all remembrance, Mnemosyne, is not simply a repository, a stone mausoleum for the storage of dead things. And the Muses are not mere attendants perpetually dusting off the coffins of forgotten events. Mnemosyne is more like a theater, upon whose stage the Muses perform what we recall of our lives. They take a person's or a people's history and shape it, re-shape it, animate it, sculpt it, draw it out, set it to music, give it color, set it free through verse, release it into the air of spoken words so that it may fly ahead to become images of the future.

While Memory is the keeper of life through remembrance, the Muses are keepers of remembrances through art. We do not talk much in our time about Mnemosyne, Memory, as a mother, preserving and protecting images of our past; still less do we call upon the Muses to make the world beautiful and joyful. Ours is a culture where the arts are considered fun but not necessary, where creativity is equated with special effects, and where the true value of artful things is determined not by their lasting ability to delight us, but by how weird and salable they are. Years ago Jung observed sadly, "The Gods have become diseases."[2] Much of what used to be recognized as the difficult gift of creative passion is now treated as curable pathology.

Mnemosyne too has become a disease: not a preserver of the memories that make our histories secure, but a disturber of our illusive and elusive peace. Now, she is thought to assault us intrusively, or elude us in a maddening way. How did once-divine Memory become a patient of modern psychotherapy, abused, disturbed, needing to be recovered and released from repression? And how is it that Memory, mother of the arts, has become a defendant in courtrooms, accused of being unreliable, distorted, manipulative, contrived, giving "false" information? When Memory is abused or mistreated – that is, taken literally, conceptualized as a filing cabinet, or computer bank for data, or as a merely mechanical function of the brain – then we *all* suffer, individually and collectively. We suffer from amnesia: loss of memoria, the capacity to make images and to see life imaginally. We suffer loss of soul.

In her book, *Pagan Grace*, Canadian scholar Ginette Paris says that "Mnemosyne is a voice, the voice of an oral culture. . . . It can come in the night as a dream, in a car as a project or longing, in bed with a lover as a sudden recollection."[3] Paris observes that memory does not just reproduce the past: it evokes a sense of meaning, it comes with poignancy, it constructs an image – which may or may not be literally true. But our culture is not an oral one anymore – talk shows and soundbites notwith-standing – and neither is it anymore a culture of the book, or written memory. We have become a culture of technological memory, a computer culture. Paris laments, "Memory more and more is restricted to accurate records and documented events, while each of us is left alone with private memories and the culture has no voice."[4]

Memory now comes to us not as the bringer of our past and compass to the future, but depersonified and mutilated into bytes that fit invisibly on floppy disks. Life is compacted to fit into ever small spaces, its bits and pieces assembled with blinding speed, a virtual reality to which we have but random access. Most of our programs are run on a hard drive, not on heart drive. Just as wisdom has been reduced to information, and thoughtful education has been reduced to learning skills, so has the goddess Mnemosyne, living memory, been reduced to a silicon chip.

In the eighteenth century, the great rabbi known as the Baal Shem Tov said, "In remembrance is the beginning of redemption." *Redemption* here comes not through sacrifice or self-denial, but through remembrance – through not letting experience be lost and forgotten. Redemption comes through being able to carry the past, however heavy the burden, because forgetting means to become uprooted, one-dimensional, flat, psychopathic. The capacity to feel deeply is in part dependent on the ability to remember *images* of deeply felt experience. One of the great advantages of growing older is that one has more history, more memories, a wealth of images stored in that living psychic temple named Mnemosyne.

Given this ancient recognition of Memory as a divinity, as the matrix of art and history, and as the beginning of redemption, we can see how American psychology's debate about false memory syndrome has been poorly framed, to the disservice of both Mnemosyne and those wounded souls who must bear her difficult images for a lifetime. The question which in recent times has generated so much heat is whether memories of childhood abuse recalled years later in adulthood are accurate recollections of literal events, or whether they are distortions: vague, confused half-fantasies, or even downright false fabrications. But of course, since all perception occurs by way of the psyche, *the psychological truth must lie in the psyche, that subjective, imaginal realm* where Mnemosyne and her daughters craft and fix their images of an individual's experience – that realm somewhere in the middle where even absolutes have blurred boundaries: the realm of "maybe," "if," and all their surrounding possibilities.

This is the realm in which psychotherapy should be done, not in a legal framework of truth or falsity. By supporting victims of childhood sexual abuse, psychotherapists of all persuasions have become involved in litigation and have often served an important function in bringing perpetrators to justice. But there has not been adequate differentiation made between the primary role of the therapist as one who attends to the soul and the very different role of one who advocates for a particular outcome in a judicial process.

There are two distinct sets of questions here, one for the courtroom and the concern for justice, and one for the consulting room and the care of the soul. They are certainly not mutually exclusive questions, but they are distinct, as "justice" and "meaning" are distinct. The requirement placed on memory in a court of law is vastly different than in a psychotherapeutic situation. Memory on the witness stand in a courtroom must be precise, linear, accurate, clear, absolutely truthful. But in the consulting room there is always a *psychological ambiguity* which preserves complexity and depth, where lived experience reveals the subtle work of the Muses in particular ways, and where such experience has multiple meanings.

We expect memory of actual events to be photographic – as if photographs always show in detail what is really there. But a photograph of anything is only a partial record, and a small part at that, for a photo captures only what the photographer sees – or wants you to see – from a single angle, in a split second of time. An alteration of shadow, air-brushing, heightened contrast, sharpness of focus or blurring: all these determine the reality portrayed in the photograph, by the photographer. If the photographer wishes, that reality may become an artistic vision rather than a factual visual record. What memory retains is the mood, the emotion, the subjective perception and experience of a reality – the psychic lens twisted a particular way – but not always the completely accurate reproduction of a literal event.

The emotional heat generated by the "false memory" debate tells us there is a powerful archetype, a deep, underlying pattern, driving it. The debate is conducted from literalized oppositional positions: we/they, us/them, abused children/abusive adults, believing therapists/skeptical theorists. The polarization of these positions is very possibly the result of the *archetype of the child* showing yet another aspect of itself in the collective psyche.

Until the middle of the twentieth century, the child archetype dominated American consciousness through its vision of limitless progress, unshadowed idealism, endless growth. This is the pubescent youngster who never grows up and thus has eternal youthful vigor and hope – always heading toward frontiers, in earlier times toward the Wild West, now to the frontiers of space; like Peter Pan, always taking the first star to the right and going straight on 'til morning. This is the child who is playful and inventive, at baseball or space stations, self-indulgent, optimistic; sometimes a bully to smaller nations, but basically a big hearty kid who unashamedly eats too fast and takes up a lot of space. At Christmas we still celebrate a sweeter aspect of the archetype, the divinity of the asexual, pure, innocent Child.

In the last decades of the twentieth century, however, the aspect of the archetype we began to see more often was the face of the child as victim: bruised and bloodied, frightened, rapidly losing hope in an adulthood worth moving toward. The archetypal child of our time is neither the gentle divine redeemer in the stable manger nor the sly pickpocketing street urchins of a Dickens tale, but the child as victim, and also the horrific visage of the child as psychopathic criminal.

The archetypal child – who by definition never grows up but merely comes to inhabit an adult body – now manifests in a nation of victimized adult children. It is no wonder that our politics, psychological theories, and therapies are developmentally arrested at a child's level. It is no wonder that those approaches which please children – causal explanations, simple solutions, literal thinking, and singularity of viewpoint – gain quick currency in modern life. Children, having short histories, have short memories. But it is part of the dignity and vocation of adulthood to remember as many events and poignant experiences and disappointments and dreams and jokes and betrayals as one can. These make up the history of a life which is more than the sum of its parts.

The substance, or sub-text, of the false memory debate concerns redemption. And what needs redemption in America, right now, is not only the child, the adult child, the family, but *Memory herself* – the faculty of imaginal memory, the capacity for holding many images of ourselves as individuals, as families, and as a people. Part of memory's redemptive value is its flexibility to remember this or that *way* – everything prefaced with a "maybe." The "maybe" helps protect us from literalizing ourselves into hard facts, keeping alive the sense of possibilities, which is perhaps the beginning of art, creativity, and imagination.

Most psychotherapists, of course, do not attempt to induce or insinuate false memories in their patients, and most patients who come to them are seeking relief from psychological pain. But to the extent that the false memory debate has fallen into the hands of literal-minded psychologists, the patient's need for psychological redemption has been turned into a demand for vindication, for confrontation and legal action. There are those few patients who come seeking not relief but revenge, through legal and social redress. They are in the wrong place. They have no questions, no maybes.

Persons who have been violated in any way need redemption, which comes through remembrance, in order to find meaning for themselves in senseless brutality. And they deserve justice, as any victim does. We have placed the burden of accomplishing both redemption and justice on memory. And by so doing, we have not respected the character of memory, which is as much a faculty of creative artfulness as it is a reliable record of events. Mnemosyne, keeper of images in the soul, is not concerned with literal truth or falsehood; still less so are her daughters, the Muses. Like the art they inspire, the Muses evoke truths of experience and wisdom, not necessarily a singular truth of fact and sworn testimony. For the Muses, as in art, truth is complex and ambiguous. And, like art, what is true may also be deceptive, and what is false may nevertheless be experienced as real. True memories have many sides, multiple meanings, blurred boundaries with facts and events. They are like the scenarios on the holodeck of the starship Enterprise – emotional reality, but not literal truth. The Muses tell the ancient Greek poet Hesiod, "We know enough to make up lies which are convincing, but we also have the skill, when we've a mind, to speak the truth."[5]

The reality of *psychic* life is that many contradictory things are true at once, and in different ways, more like in dreams than in data reports. In the imaginal realm, most things prove false at one time or another in different ways. There is always a maybe. Maybe it was this way and meant that; or maybe it was that way and meant this. Maybe it was, and maybe it wasn't – but what the soul wants to know is what it would mean either way. How would my life be different if I remembered or forgot? How would I be different if I remembered an event from my childhood in a particular way, attaching a particular meaning, than if I remembered the same event with a different meaning? How would I be different if I forgot a particular childhood event entirely?

These are questions for psychotherapy; they are therapeutic questions because, like the Muses, they attend to the real needs of the wounded soul. They seek redemption through the art of making remembered experience meaningful. Since they are not legal questions, they shift the false memory debate from the courtroom to the consulting room. More importantly, these kinds of questions move the experiences of a painful childhood to an arena where the child need no longer be crucified between opposite poles: not absolutes of victim/perpetrator, abused/abuser, child/adult, right/wrong, innocent/guilty, on and on.

Confronting one's abuser, family, spouse, may indeed lead to some sort of redemption. But in attending to the soul's deepest need, the essential question is not so much *what* I remember, but *how* I remember it.[6] How has such a memory image given form to my life? How has it helped form my character? How have I been psychologically *de*formed by such a memory image? How has it encouraged, or ruined, my ability to trust, to think well of myself, to love? To redeem the memory image means to find meaning in it. This is what makes the future possible. Elie

Wiesel, Holocaust survivor, once said, "Memory is the possibility of becoming more of a human being. Memory is a way of redeeming your past. Memory is for the sake, not of the dead, but of the future."[7]

In the old days in Greece, the Muse named Clio was the matrix and crafter of history, which was imagined not as a chronological sequence of literal events, but as a great epic of human entanglements with Fate and divinities. The Muses create history by shaping and preserving images of what has happened, or more accurately, what has been *experienced*. Clio's task, with her musing sisters, is to craft or paint or narrate a pattern of a life where one can see the entanglements.

In a real sense, the purpose of deep soul work is to reveal the unfolding pattern of one's life as a series of divine interventions, or intrusions, from those archetypal powers that govern the soul. Each of us can remember moments when it felt as though some divinity, some unseen hand, moved to turn events a certain way – a letter sent too late, a wrong turn that led to a strange opportunity, a single intuitive decision that changed the course of a life, a sudden impulse that destroyed something of great value, an inheritance that came in the nick of time, a chance meeting that became a romance. The big and the small of one's life may be felt as equally fateful, all woven into the tapestry that gives each individual life its own unique design.

In the beginning, there were three goddesses, the Fates: one to spin the thread of life, one to measure it, one to cut it. Not only mortals, but even the gods were subject to the decrees of Fate. But the ancient Greeks had a saying that *the Muses – and only the Muses – can change the weave of Fate.* This is a remarkable psychological idea, and a redemptive one, for it suggests that one is never trapped by one's fate, never permanently imprisoned in the pain of one's childhood, never completely bound by the limitations of one's present circumstance.

What brings redemption and freedom from the heavy hand of Fate is not the frenetic activity of data-gathering, and not a heroic egotistic attitude that tries to break down all barriers, all limitations, trampling over one's history in the determination to dictate all the terms of one's life. No, what brings real change, real redemption from the entrapment in the deadening sense of fatalism that stops all creativity, are the Muses. These beautiful daughters of Mnemosyne are able to take the most horrific and anguished experiences of our lives and work their artistry upon them. The Muses enable us to make poetry from pain, lyric from loneliness, literature from personal tragedy. This is what releases us from the sense of meaninglessness that keeps us stuck in pain.

Please note: the Muses cannot undo the horror of brutal childhoods nor minimize the anguish of loss and grief; but they can change the pattern of how one perceives and responds to what Shakespeare called the "thousand natural shocks that flesh is heir to." In other words, the Muses spin the thread of which our lives are made; the threads of experience cannot be changed – but the Muses can change the way the design of that fabric is woven.

The Muses can change the psychological design of one's life because, if we allow them, they inspire us to work with the images that live in our memories; they inspire us – and sometimes *drive* us – to search for a sense of continuity and meaning in what has happened to us. Through our memory images, the Muses show us where we have been, help us reflect on where we are, and muse imaginatively on where we are going. As Mnemosyne is the keeper of the psychic archives that keep our history intact, so her offspring the Muses use the archives as the raw material from which to fashion images that return us to who we are and turn us toward what we might become.

Psychological history is different from literal history, in that it is a collection of images made from subjective experience and not exclusively from external events. It is the difference between an impressionist's painting and a journalist's photograph. Memory and imagination go together; the one is hardly possibly without the other. Mnemosyne is not much interested in mere record keeping, faultless accounts – nor accountability. She is concerned with imaginal life, the life and preservation of images. Above all, she is devoted to remembering the gods, the powers, the ideas, or the archetypes that form the patterns of our lives.

Modern Americans, in particular, have a distinct dislike and distrust of history. And our conception of the human psyche is a reductive, materialistic one. So Jung's startling idea that "image is psyche" is practically incomprehensible to us (except to confirm our collective suspicion that Jung was something of a mystical eccentric and not to be taken seriously). Our sense of history is reduced to the recollection of literal facts. And this is where the false memory debate has led us astray, for the recollection of literal facts can never bring genuine healing to a wounded soul. The soul does not want mere recollection, literalism, or certainty; it wants living images full of emotion; it wants art that evokes these emotions; it wants history solidified as remembrance. And the soul wants redemption.

Our modern ability to remember has been so atrophied, our sense of history so foreshortened, that the idea of "ancient" now applies to anything that happened a few years ago. (Recently I heard a sportscaster on

television refer to a record that was set "way back in 1999". This, relatively, would put *my* childhood somewhere back in the Middle Ages). It
was way, *way* back in the mid-1980s (I think) that the so-called "false
memory syndrome" debate began to gain currency in the national
awareness of child abuse and the role of psychotherapists treating adults.
From the beginning, the debate focused almost entirely on the question
of the correctness of recall of incidents that might have happened in
childhood.

The controversy over repressed memories turns not only on the
accuracy of memory, but also expects that incidents of childhood abuse
about which one might have a true or false memory are of a sexual nature.
This alone should make us stop and wonder why we assume that *sexual*
experiences are so much more harmful to children than continual verbal
condemnations from parents, public racial slurs and humiliations from
schoolmates or teachers, or force-fed religious and ethnic bigotry from the
child's community. All of these childhood experiences constitute "child
abuse," and each of them is a violation, a violence perpetrated upon
children that leaves scars for life. Some may be even deeper than those we
expect from sexual trauma.

From the deep perspective of the psyche, *the most pressing question
in the debate is not about the accuracy of memory but about the
interpretation of what has been experienced.* And in soul work what has
been experienced is a matter for interpretation, not verification. What does
it matter that a woman or a man in pain comes to therapy and remembers,
thinks they remember, isn't sure they remember, wants to or doesn't want
to remember, that they were sexually approached, coached, touched,
seduced, molested, or raped twenty, thirty, forty years ago?

It matters greatly because they say it does. It matters because for human
beings the subjective reality of pain and emotion has primacy of value
and importance. It matters because their psychic experience is real, and
true, even though it may not be perfectly factual. It matters because their
experience and their interpretation of it continues to affect the course of
their psychic, social, sexual, and physical lives.

The Muses, divine daughters of Memory, shape experience into images
and then, like true artists, preserve them in such a way that neither time
nor neglect will destroy their substance. The importance of the Muses in
human life is every bit as important as Mother Memory. For while it is
Memory that records, it is the Muses who give meaning to the record.
This is why we may have only a vague, fleeting memory of the literal
circumstances of a long-past event, but the emotions attached to that wisp
of memory are still sharp, piercing, lodged permanently and precisely in

the imagination and in the body. And it is with these emotions that the Muses must work to create new meaning, not only to relieve the pain, but to redirect the psyche's creativity so that we may get on with life.

Once the episodes and/or climate of an abusive childhood have been recalled and made part of conscious life, it is not necessarily useful just to recall and rehearse the actual details, over and over again, year after year. The problem is how to stop living *in* and *from* that wound and how to start living *with* it. Redemption *begins* in remembrance, but its *continuing* effect depends on the ability of the one who remembers to imagine forwardly, to call again upon those *possibilities* for one's life *that have not yet been considered or allowed into consciousness*. No one is only one-dimensional; no one is only a victim.

A careful therapy of an adult who was wounded as a child requires not just regression to recall and relive the wound; it also requires progression through remembrance of what that child has, and might have otherwise, become. This is a remembrance not of all that was true or false, but of all the maybes, the thousand maybes and might-have-beens. As long as that early painful experience remains the central and defining experience of one's life, no real creativity is possible; life is lived in reruns – no new ideas, no new characters, no new plots, no new possibilities.

This is not blaming the victim. It is rather de-victimizing the person who has suffered painful blows in childhood; it is a refusal to tag the person with an eternal label of "victim," a label of choice for too many therapy clients. This label has been handed out by psychologists, journalists, and lawyers, who keep referring to such persons as victims – not as adults, not as individuals who have experienced anything else, not as persons, but as victims. The Muses assist us to *dis*identify with the victim archetype by calling us to reshape the context and import of those experiences of childhood which wounded us, so that we may honor the wound without having to suffer it daily, centrally, eternally.

You cannot look at Michelangelo's sculptures or read Maya Angelou's writings and *know* for certain whether they were abused as children. What matters is what they have made, the enduring images in stone and words they have given the world. Their works are full of suffering and power and so they speak to everyone, regardless of personal history or individual circumstance. But we know that Michelangelo suffered all his life from the mean-spirited and self-serving manipulation of his father, and we know that Maya Angelou had endured enough shattering pain by the time she was ten to fill a lifetime. But Maya Angelou is not a victim: she was our national Poet Laureate. And Michelangelo became immortal when he first struck chisel to stone.

They did not live *in* their wounds, nor *from* them, but *with* them, and from those tortured memories gave us beauty. It is not necessary to remember accurately, or even literally; it is enough that one remembers imaginally, carries images embodying an experience of childhood pain. Most of us have little or no particular artistic inclination or talent – nor do we need it. The Muses are not élitist. They do not compare a person who sings off-key in the shower with one who performs with the Metropolitan Opera. They do not decide that one person's crude stick figure drawing is less worthy than a Rembrandt painting. What matters is that we reflect on our experience *as if* we had the eye of an artist – that we wonder, muse, ponder the ways we could render and interpret our experiences. The Muses are not interested in legal or objective truth or scientific accuracy; they are interested in making life-sustaining images that express what has happened to us. These are the deepest images that give us voice.

Perhaps the greatest gift of the Muses is the restoration of language to those rendered mute and inarticulate by violence. Trauma makes one speechless; the full horror and violation of personhood that victims suffer cannot be expressed in words. To lose the ability to speak, to tell one's story, is to be condemned to hell, which is solitary confinement in silence. Elie Wiesel, Auschwitz survivor at fifteen, stayed silent, locked in his memory with unbearable images, for ten years after his rescue from the death camp. Maya Angelou, raped at seven, became completely mute for years. A thirty-eight-year-old man I see now in analysis, accomplished, educated, successful, speaks for the first time in thirty years about humiliating sexual molestation in grade school. A woman I have worked with for nearly four years, a psychotherapist who was herself sexually violated twice as a young girl, began to write her dreams and therein found a language to express her reality. For each of these people, and countless more, remembrance in the form of speech means the beginning of redemption.

Redemption, however, is not the same as justice. The false memory argument has confused the two, assuming that legal action accomplishes psychological redemption. Acting from this assumption, the first impulse is to *externalize* a person's past experience into an interpersonal confrontation with the perpetrator – before it is fully understood how the experience has been psychologically formative. And the second impulse is to *literalize* the memory of abuse and take the perpetrator to court.

There is no doubt that the need for justice in human affairs is as essential as the need for food; but the kind of justice a victim may expect from the legal system is not remotely adequate to bring about genuine healing or permanent change in the person who has been wronged. This kind of healing and change, since it is of a psychological nature, must happen in the psyche, in the interior. *One must come to terms with one's experience.* In this sense, justice is only a part of the therapeutic process, and possibly not the first part.

The child in the psyche wants a return to innocence, a return to a time before wounding. It does not want redemption, it wants injury undone, bad things and bad people banished. No amount of justice or confrontation with literal perpetrators, no apologies from the abuser, no monetary satisfaction from successful lawsuits and no therapeutic assurances can *truly* bring the end to pain that the child longs for. But those who are receptive to the Muses – not only those who have some remarkable talent, but those who suffer and need the consolation of art and imagination – are the ones who are touched by the Muses. They have the chance somehow to refashion their hurtful histories into future visions.

We have thought that the way to stop the cycle of violence – abused children who become abusive adults who raise abused children – is to provide education and jobs and economic opportunities for young people, to give them dignity and independence, replacing anger and despair. Of course we *must* do this. But what is needed just as desperately, just as deeply, is cultural sanction for art, and a wider appreciation for what constitutes human art forms: not only music, literature, painting, sculpture, but also the amazing poetry of seven-year-olds, old recipes for bread and homemade wine, the crafting of a friendship that lasts a lifetime, the patient work that culminates in the stunning beauty of a racehorse coming to the wire, and cultivation of one's garden that brings joy to all who see it.

Art is not just a product; it is an attitude. Artistry is not just skill and training; it is an approach to life. The necessity of art in and for human life is partly demonstrated by its antiquity: we do not know of a time in human existence when there was no art. Witness the prehistoric cave paintings in France, which suggest that from the dawn of humanity activity and art belonged together: pictures of animals made by hunters for whom the hunt *and* its portrayal were practically the same thing. And art certainly does not come only from the sweetly young and innocent, those untouched by tragedy. The greatest art often is born from pain and sorrow, for this is what makes pain and sorrow endurable, and even, sometimes, transformative.

It is important that we learn to remember forwardly as well as remembering what is past. We find this idea, in passing, in one of the great psychological texts of the nineteenth century, Lewis Carroll's *Alice in*

Wonderland, where the laws of time and space are reversed or irrelevant. The White Queen observes that Alice has a terribly linear, and much too limited, notion of memory. Alice, who can only remember what is past, says of her memory, "I'm sure *mine* only works one way. I can't remember things *before* they happen." And the Queen remarks, "It's a poor sort of memory that only works backwards." Though confused, little Alice asks, "What sort of things do *you* remember best?" "Oh, things that happened the week after next," the Queen replies in a careless tone.

The White Queen is right: it is a poor sort of memory, a poor sort of imaginal memory, that only works backwards. There is an art to remembering forwardly, to anticipating with passion what one can be or do in life. It requires an image, or many images. As the Muses craft history into epic poems, so may a single person craft his or her history – a case history of one's own – into a lived poem, a life full of all kinds of memory images – ugly memories, joyful memories, sorrowful and painful memories, funny and embarrassing and ridiculous memories, sensate memories of how some things felt even when it can't be remembered how it actually was, or if it ever *really* was. In the course of psychic life, literal events by themselves count for relatively little. Look at the paucity of literal events in the life of Emily Dickinson, or Marcel Proust, who spent years in bed engaging in a remembrance of things past. The memory of an experience, the image of the emotions we experience, this is everything, for the image is where the soul resides.

I leave with you a Jewish story. In times past, when the great rabbi, Baal Shem Tov, the Master of the Good Name, had a problem, it was his custom to go to a certain part of the forest. There he would light a fire, say a prayer, and find wisdom. A generation later, a son of one of his disciples was in the same position. He went to that same place in the forest and lit the fire, but he could not remember the prayer. However, he asked for wisdom and that was enough for him to find what he needed. A generation after that, his son had a problem like his predecessors. He also went to the forest, but he could not even light the fire. "Lord," he prayed, "I cannot remember the prayer and I cannot get the fire started. But I am in the forest. That will have to be sufficient." And it was. Now, Rabbi Ben Levi sits in his study in Minneapolis, his head in his hands, and prays, "Lord, look at us now. We have forgotten the prayer. The fire is out. We can't find our way back to the place in the forest. We can only remember that there was a fire, a prayer, a place in the forest. So Lord, now that must be sufficient."[8]

And it is.

Notes

1. Patricia Hampl, "Memory and Imagination," in James McConkey (ed.), *The Anatomy of Memory*, New York: Oxford University Press, 1996, p. 210.
2. C.G. Jung, *Alchemical Studies*, *Collected Works*, vol. 13, New Jersey: Princeton University Press, 1967, para. 54.
3. Ginette Paris, *Pagan Grace*, Dallas: Spring Publications, Inc., 1990, p. 121.
4. Ibid., p. 125.
5. Hesiod, *Theogony*, translated by Dorothea Wender, London: Penguin, 1973, ll. 27–9.
6. See James Hillman and Michael Ventura, *We've Had A Hundred Years of Psychotherapy and the World's Getting Worse*, New York: HarperCollins, 1992 , pp. 22ff.
7. Elie Wiesel, television interview, *c.*1996.
8. I first came across this story many years ago in Barbara Myerhoff's wonderful book, *Number Our Days*, New York: Simon & Schuster, 1980, p. 112.

Chapter 6

Styx and stones

Hatred and the art of cursing

I hate standing in line at the grocery store. I hate it when drivers drive slowly in the left lane. It burns me up when I call with a question about my health insurance and get a menu that takes twenty minutes and has more numbered options than I have on my telephone. I become enraged when I can't open a package of flashlight batteries without tools because they are impenetrably, seamlessly sealed in hard plastic.

These are not exactly situations of cosmic import. These situations are just that – *situations* that frustrate, anger, annoy, irritate and drive me temporarily insane. But strictly speaking, and speaking psychologically, they have nothing to do, really, with hatred – even though some of the curses I have formulated in these situations over the years are quite eloquent and possibly classic. These sorts of events are part of the daily life endured by most of us most of the time, and so they do not define us in an individual way.

Slow checkout lines and bad driving and sadistic packaging are mere lead-ins to a more subversive view of hatred, a view from the turned-under side. The soul is not just about love and warmth; it also has the capacity for deep, implacable hatred and regions that are frozen and do not melt at the warmth of human touch. While psychotherapy tries to help us love more and better, it usually ignores the possibility that we are defined as much by who and what we hate as by who and what we love. Love is both method and goal of therapy; hatred can be neither.

I like love as much as anyone. But just because I like it so much, my inclination to subversion compels me to question its underside, and the underside of love is hatred – not indifference, which lacks intensity, but hatred, which is as powerful and passionate and intense as real love. I've always found it liberating that, unlike most other psychotherapeutic approaches and the theories that inform them, depth psychology is not interested in moral improvement, and therefore is able to give equal attention to hatred while simultaneously attending to the needs of love.

Hatred has gotten such bad press for so long that we have come to believe that any kind of hatred is bad. Love and forgiveness and understanding are the good stuff we are required to give other people. But hatred ought to have equal time; even the Bible suggests this. These are the words of Ecclesiastes the Preacher, son of David, king in Jerusalem: "For everything there is a season, and a time for everything under heaven: a time to be born, and a time to die; a time to kill, and a time to heal; a time to break down, and a time to build up; a time to embrace, and a time to refrain from embracing; a time to keep silence, and a time to speak; a time to love, and a time to hate."[1]

There is a time for hatred, says the Bible, a necessary, God-appointed time. Hatred is one of the fundamentals of human life, for which there is a time and proper place. It is not some sort of spiritual disease that turns a few into sadistic psychopaths and ultra-right-wing bigots. We all feel it, at some time, but most of us have trouble placing it properly.

And yet, by considering hatred as a just-so reality, by placing it in the same category of necessities as birth, death, speaking, and loving, there is already a protest against it forming within us, a resistance. Hatred, we have been taught, isn't nice. We have been taught that hatred and rejection go together somehow, and that if we hate somebody they will feel rejected and probably take up a life of crime or sexual perversion, or, worse, their feelings will be hurt. No one who is not a psychopath wants to assume the heavy moral burden of rejecting another through hatred – it not only presumably drives the hated one into depravity, it also wrecks your own self-image of reasonable decency.

So any dignifying of hatred, even with biblical sanction, flies in the face of all collective morality and two millenia of collective ethical values, beginning with the teachings of Jesus, who urged us to love our enemies and pray for those who persecute us. How can we possibly imagine that hatred should be accorded a rightful place among other human necessities, such as being born and healing and embracing and loving? How can we speak of its necessity without seeming to advocate it? Having lost its rightful place in our scale of values, hatred restored seems like hatred exalted. But of course, if I appear to be exalting hatred, it only shows the extent to which the hatred of which we are capable has been denied or repressed. When hatred returns, as the repressed always does, it returns with a vengeance, and often in the form of vengeance.

Hatred is obviously a problem of what Jung called the "shadow," but I don't want to deflect too far into shadow talk because we will lose the specificity and immediacy of hatred when it rises from the soul's core.[2] The shadow tends to be subsumed under the rubric of "individuation" – meaning it must be integrated into the larger Self – and usually evokes notions of serious unpleasantries but nothing that can't be handled by a sturdy ego. The big items, such as sadistic psychopathy, sexual violence, racism, sexism, and hatred, are just some of the shadow contents that are usually talked about in generalizations, and so they are hard to see in ourselves.

Hatred poses a particular problem, though, in that it is most strongly prohibited, the biggest of all moral no-no's. Even when we condemn people who do hateful things, such as psychopathic criminals or sexual predators, we are forbidden to enjoy the punishment of evildoers or take pleasure in their downfall. That would reduce us, would make Us just like Them, the good no better than the bad.

But shadows are in collusion with each other; there is always an affinity between the good and the bad, otherwise how would we recognize either? What fascinates may also repel, and whatever is our highest value is also our lowest level of compulsion. If I come to hate the hatred I feel toward those who are worthy of hate, I know then that I've been caught in a defensive trap and must refuse recognition that there is a terrible but true point of identity between myself and the one I hate.

Hatred is not only, or even primarily, about being good and bad; it is about being ugly. Hatred is clearly and sharply ugly. Some of its ugliness is instantly recognizable: the ugliness of red swastikas painted on synagogues, of burning crosses and white sheets of the Ku Klux Klan, the cold, impassive faces of the Puritan fathers as they burned hell out of witches in old Salem.

Hatred is also stupid. It is an attitude based on stupid ideas about racial or religious or sexual superiority. At the time of writing, there are more than 2,000 websites on the Internet that promote this sort of stupidity and ugliness. My personal hostility towards these sites is not because they lack decency (which may also be said of half the politicians now holding office), but because they pollute the intellectual environment with excremental stupidity, and there is already enough shit in the world.

The psychological work of finding some redeeming value in hatred becomes all the more important since we have only a one-sided view of it, that it is ugly and stupid. And it will not go away. So it is absolutely necessary that the veneer of piety that obscures our experience of the depth and quality and range and vitality of hatred be stripped away. If for no other reason, we cannot afford not to: *survival* depends on it. Denial of hatred, and fear of hatred, merely puts us at the mercy of those who know their hatred and are not afraid of it. It is not the *number* of bombs in the world's nuclear arsenal that is so terrifying; it is knowing that they can be used, intentionally, with malice aforethought. It is a lie for Americans to insist that we will never be guilty of a first strike because we are a peaceloving nation and harbor only goodwill to the world. The world does not believe this and neither should we. The image on World War I posters of bloodthirsty Huns and World War II pictures of leering Japanese were at least honest, if not accurate.

We do not know, in agonizing detail and depth, just what we hate, nor how we hate. But it is possible that if we take time to hate well, and give hatred enough rightful time and attention, we may begin to mitigate some of the actual violence in our world – not all of which is physical – and to slake some of the thirst for vengeance which Christianity would deny us and which makes intentional violence in all forms so characteristic of our time.

Now, if I speak *for* hatred, I am not speaking *against* love. These experiences are independent of each other, but not mutually exclusive. They are not true opposites but rather complement each other, being woven of different but equally intensely colored, passionate fibers, and therefore where one thrives, the other may prosper also. For everything there is a season. And yet, we clearly do not accord the same importance to hatred as we do to love. Hatred, then, needs more attention, and we need to be able to hate more openly. Not more actively, just more openly. Like much of what belongs to the *un*integratable shadow, we have tried to keep hatred in the closet; but the closet has never been a good place for storing hatred because things lose *definition* in the dark.

Consider: why should love get all the attention, all the roses, all the valentines? After all, love needs hatred to deepen itself and give it stability. Why should hatred not be a point of reference as love is? Yet there is no question that, as a culture, our preference lies with love, at least consciously. Our religions, our welfare programs, our psychologies, our criteria for relationships, are all informed by the ideal of love. And when love is the ideal, it refers less to sexual love than to the idealized Christian vision of asexual, altruistic love. Listen to St. Paul: Love is patient and kind; love is not jealous or boastful; it is not arrogant or rude. Love does not insist on its own way; it is not irritable or resentful; it does not rejoice at wrong, but rejoices in the right. "Love bears all things, believes all things, hopes all things, endures all things. Love never ends. . . . Make love your aim . . . "[3]

We may not think of love consciously in these terms anymore; we are more likely to think of love in terms of sex, and feeling good, and being comfortable, and having our needs met, and perhaps passion, and the jealousy that accompanies difficult love affairs and deep relationships. But precisely because we are not likely to think of it, this view of love as articulated in St. Paul needs to be brought forth, because our conscious attitudes toward the whole range of love, from complex sexuality to passing common courtesy, are informed by it unconsciously. In short, modern American ideas about love, however debased at times, rest on this Christian foundation. St. Paul is a tough act to follow.

Love has always gotten good press throughout history, especially since Jesus was proclaimed the incarnation of it. And it is still the highest value, even if its power to inspire seems to have dimmed a little. We do not have the incarnation of love amongst us anymore, but we do have its preachers and poets and psychotherapists. People write books and more books about love: how to love, when to love, whom to love, the nature of love; country music is all about broken love and splendid love, and grocery stores sell novels of love along with potatoes and peanut butter. Love sells, and we are sold on it.

But love, so prevalent, so exalted, is also our deepest pathology; and indeed this is the profound horror: that love *may* inspire and motivate more cruelty and pain than hatred ever could. Sticks and stones may break my bones, but love can surely kill me. For the *love* of God the Crusaders slaughtered their way to Jerusalem. For *love* of the Fatherland and purity of blood the Third Reich was built on human bones and ashes. For love, the romantic poet will fall into black despair, take sick, even die. Martyrs of every faith die for love. A man inflamed with jealousy will murder his beloved and his plea in court will be insanity by reason of love, the madness of passionate love.

So you see, love is the problem. Having been raised to the highest value in our culture, it is responsible for our worst degradations. Jealous murders, sexual violence, therapeutic malpractice, fanatic persecutions and character assassinations are all done in its name – and done with at least partial sanction of our religious and moral convictions. For we do not accord divinity to hatred, but we all know that God is Love.

To give hatred equal time, as Ecclesiastes does, means also to give hatred equality with other emotions and attitudes. To find our way back to this status of equality – for love was not always the single ruling divinity – I want to go back in psychological time, which is not linear or chronological, but is marked qualitatively by the depth and interiority of experiences. In other words, I want to revert to the mythic realm, a realm of origins with stories of beginnings.

There are others, but I am choosing a story told by Hesiod, the Greek poet. I choose him because he tells a good story, and because he is inspired, and he knows that there is a time to love and a time to hate – and that the two do not necessarily have anything to do with each other.

Modern humanistic psychology would have us place a minus sign before hatred and call it "negative," as if hatred was just an accidental insufficiency or deficit of the positive, love. But there was a time when hatred was not merely the insubstantial pale shadow of lovelessness. Before words had lost much of their meaning and power to move, hatred could be spoken, articulated, pronounced – in the form of a curse – and the effect was as forceful as any physical weapon. Sticks and stones may break my bones, but words can truly kill me. This is the story that Hesiod tells in the *Theogony*. Deep in the darkness of the Underworld,

> there lives the goddess hated by the gods, Terrible Styx, daughter of Ocean, who flows back upon himself. Far from the gods she has her famous home roofed-over with great rocks. Sometimes when fights and quarrelling arise among the gods and some of the gods tell a lie, then Zeus sends Iris with a golden jug to fetch the sacred stuff by which gods swear an oath, the famous chilly water which flows down from the high precipice. . . . One tenth of [Ocean] is given to her. Winding about the earth, he has nine streams with silver eddies, and he falls again into the salty main; only this one, Styx, flows from a rock, great burden to the gods.[4]

The name of this goddess, Styx, is associated with the Greek word *stygein*, which means "to hate," and carries the sense of darkness, gloom, and depth. "Stygian" also means something inviolable or irrevocable. Styx is not only the oldest of the daughters of Ocean and Tethys, she is also the mightiest. Styx received her honored place as Oath of the Gods as a reward from Zeus, for she was the first to join with him against the Titans, sending him two of her children, Kratos and Bia, Strength and Force. And we might note here that one of the services hatred performs is to help subdue the titanic delusions that love is enough, that goodwill will save us, and that the "unconscious" is, mostly, happily creative.

We have an image here of not just love as flow and peace like a river, as an old hymn sings, but also the unrelenting flow of hatred in its own time and season and from its own source, the mighty river carrying in its current the power of curse. Styx flows from a rock, the only river of Ocean to do so, as if hatred originates in some solid, implacable, intransigent place in the soul. As the Church of Christ is built immovable upon a rock, so does the sacred Oath, by which all the gods swear, issue from a rock.

Like the Bible in today's courtroom, like the testicles of Hebrew men in ancient times, the river Styx – the honored, the hated – is a holy foundation of sworn testimony, the arbiter of and witness to truth. Love is not the foundation of the gods' justice: hatred is.

Hatred is the proper and inevitable response to injustice. Just as hatred is the foundation of the gods' justice, so it may be our foundation to realize justice, to make justice real. I am not talking here about justice in abstract terms – as an attribute of deity, as a function of law, or as an ideal goal of moral evolution. I am talking about justice as an absolute requirement for life, like food or sleep. After all, the worst crimes against humanity, including slavery in the American south, apartheid in South Africa, ethnic and religious atrocities around the globe, have been committed with the conviction of divine righteousness, with legal sanction, and in the name of morality.

All through human history the anguished cry of the oppressed and tormented soul has been sent to Heaven, praying for relief, comfort, revenge, and above all, for justice. The demand for justice often takes the form of a curse, carefully crafted, with great attention to the detailed destruction desired for the enemy, grand and eloquent in its absolute bitterness. We should hardly think it unusual – certainly not pathological – when a victim pronounces a curse on those who have enslaved, tortured, brutalized, exploited, robbed, raped, and murdered. Curse-prayers insist that God fulfill his role as Judge: may the enemy be stricken with dis-figurement and disease, may he see his children starve to death, may he lose his livelihood and all material goods, may his house fall down on his head, may he be exiled and penniless, may he have mud and stones thrown at him, may his name and memory be obliterated forever, may he spend all the nights of eternity in hell.

Love is not enough. In fact, love is not the point here at all. While we are busy with love – wishing for its presence, lamenting its absence, complaining of its quality, suffering its beauty – the psychological work is being done in the Underworld, at the periphery, at the outermost boundary where hatred runs her course. Beyond our vision, but at impassable boundaries of our souls, hatred preserves the soul, encircling it in a frigid embrace, doing its own work of preserving passion for justice and protecting truth.

When I speak of "truth" and "truthfulness" here, I do not mean it in the sense of a moral or legal or historical truth. I do not mean truth as a collective moral value or as literal fact. Truth is not necessarily fact, just as facts may, in some sense, "lie." I mean "truth" in the sense of personal integrity, an accurate presentation of your character.

Like a bell that rings true, the truth that hatred supports refers to the accuracy, precision, and exactness of one's conscience. There are often times when, in the absence of such accuracy, one is telling a lie, missing the mark, being untrue – as in reporting only part of an event; in revealing a secret without its context; or in the interior evasion of deep feeling. But well-differentiated hatred may be an encouraging antidote to Hamlet's glum observation that "conscience doth make cowards of us all." Hatred's work of protecting truth gives the soul courage, and preserves its integrity.

The preserving quality of hatred is in its coldness; it freezes what needs to be kept forever, makes passion freeze into a rock of ice. It does not melt away into slushy formless puddles of sentimentality. The hatred of which we are *conscious* may be only the tip of the iceberg. Beneath that, at bottom, flows the frigid river Styx.

One of the works that hatred does then, psychologically, is a work of differentiation. Love, we all know, is blind, or at least myopic, but hatred sees with a cold, penetrating glare into the truth of a matter. The better one hates – note, I said "better," not "more" – the more refined one's hatred becomes, it is placed more discriminately, used more precisely to cut away falseness and clichés and façades, it is wrought with greater intellectual clarity. Hatred requires an exactitude of inflection and nuance. And hatred must be specific, so that specific loves and values may be protected from lies.

Cosmic loving, as in "I-love-humanity," is as useless and ridiculous as "I-hate-Jews (Catholics, Blacks, gays, telemarketers, whatever your group preference)." One needs to give careful attention to one's hatreds, as to one's loves. I am afraid of people who love indiscriminately. It means they do not choose their lovers carefully, and therefore they may hate anyone with the same indiscriminate projection. I am especially terrified of evangelistic Christian love, however fundamental, precisely because it is so fundamentally all-embracing. Such an all-inclusive embrace smothers my individuality. At bottom, I am not loved for my uniqueness, but for my creatureliness, a condition I share with anonymous billions as the lowest common denominator. I object to undiscriminating, mindless love because it ignores my mind. This sort of love, that perceives no differences, wants salvation above all, and does not change, is deadly. It is like the vampire's night-kiss, demanding more and more, slowly sucking the vitality of discriminating hatred out of the soul, so that the deep river that coldly preserves one's individual truth runs dry. Whoever does not take time to sit reflectively on the banks of the great river Styx does not know her own individual boundaries, nor the great power and depth of her own soul.

Just as we ought not to love indiscriminately, nor eat indiscriminately, nor grieve indiscriminately, neither should we hate indiscriminately. And it seems to me that if we took time to discriminate amongst our hatreds, there would be less need to practice discrimination against actual persons. In Shakespeare's *The Merchant of Venice* is a fine example of differentiated hatred, and it comes from the one who is hated *in*discriminately as a member of a despised group. The Jew Shylock is invited to dinner by an enemy, and he answers: "I will buy with you, sell with you, talk with you, walk with you, and so following; but I will not eat with you, drink with you, nor pray with you."[5]

How wonderfully subtle, yet clear, is Shylock's hatred! The deepest values that most closely touch our truth or integrity are expressed in sacramental activities like eating, drinking, or praying – and these are exactly the spheres from which the enemy is to be excluded, denied access to the private and vulnerable places in one's soul. This holding to oneself – *not sharing* – gives precision and exact shape to one's values. To my enemy I say, I will attend a meeting with you but I will not have a drink with you afterward. I will do all manner of business with you, but I will not invite you into my home. I will work personally with you as a colleague but I will not be known to you privately. I will attend an arms reduction treaty talk with you, but I will not love you. It is *not* at all the case that I am *trying* to love you and wish to protect you from my own nasty shadow projections. It *is* that I hate you and *dare not perjure myself* by pretending that I do not. My real life is hidden away and protected by Styx, not given over to my enemy, not exposed in the marketplace of the world to be misconstrued, or prostituted, or converted, not lost in empty words that pretend friendship and thus demean my *true* friends. For the sake of my integrity, I swear by Great Styx, I will not allow my enemy to see those things in me I hold most dear, for then I have cast my pearls before swine.

The art of cursing is a means of differentiating hatred, one of the best means in fact, because the formulation of a curse is the precise articulation of hatred. The articulation of a curse both clarifies and gives power to the one who pronounces it, for a psychologically effective curse requires intimate knowledge of the enemy, and knowledge is power.

I am not thinking of the careless, offhand sorts of curses we throw around daily. These are empty curses, not mindful of the gods. Effective cursing requires imagination, and this in turn requires a discipline of specificity and precision. If you are content to go around with an indiscriminate "damn" all the time, merely directing everyone merely to go to hell, this is not really serious cursing; it is just spleen venting, sloppy irritability, and no one takes you seriously when you say it. A curse should be as specific as possible. Here is a favorite of mine from ancient Greece, which pronounces a curse for the protection of a tomb: "Whoever digs here, may his face be scraped with an iron broom; and so also with him who advised him to it."[6] A longer, more comprehensive curse was fashioned also for the protection of a tomb, its marker, and its contents. (So we have the truth, the whole truth, and quite a lot of the truth.)

> May God smite him with distress and fever and chills and itch and blight and madness and blindness and starting out of his wits; and may his possessions disappear, neither may he walk on the land nor sail on the sea nor beget children; may his house not increase, neither may he enjoy produce, nor his house, nor daylight, nor the use nor possession of anything.[7]

The art of cursing has fallen on hard times; good feelings get all the attention, as we learn to share how we feel about this and that (whether or not anyone else cares). But hardly anyone bothers much with the craft of cursing, and it has never really been part of the American way, perhaps because of the Puritan influence that so deeply pervades our culture. In contrast, the Irish and Italians and Greeks have always been wonderful curse-makers. It is a tradition that keeps alive both the older sense of craft and precision in knowing your enemies, of keeping the ancient sense that the gods are at work in this feud, this enmity, this curse being wrought in iron. And it is a tradition that keeps alive the psychological realization that at some deep level, *what we call human hatred is also the wrath of God*. Again, the pronouncement of a curse is a demand for justice.

We forget, or repress, or are embarrassed by, our profound power to hate and to call down curses on our fellow mortals. This is because we have forgotten or repressed – lost faith in – those deep archetypal realities, or gods, who fill us with their visions and power. We do not really take cursing seriously as an act of individual power, any more than we have real faith in blessing, which in the modern world has been replaced with secular good luck or vibes. But beneath this, we *fear* this power and what it might do if unleashed, even if only in the warheads of words. There is an archaic, primitive, and barbaric soul in each of us, a soul that remembers the gods and fears their power. To the extent that we fear power and hate hatred, to that extent we are rendered powerless and deprived of our inner authority to affirm the truths of our own souls.

A curse that is pronounced from one's integrity, from the depth of one's hatred, is as hard and unbreakable and permanent as a rock, like the

Church, or like a millstone around the neck. Cursing is a use of individual power which must be cared for so that the power is not squandered or abused.

In therapy circles everywhere one hears people complaining that they hate themselves and want to stop. They want, in the jargon of today, to "give themselves permission" to do this or that, to "be all that they can be," as the United States Army promises, they want to be free to grow, etc., none of which they can do because they feel crippled and shackled by self-hatred. They think, as we all do, that the way out is to stop hating so much. But this is not a psychological answer, and not a very creative one, either.

One very good way out of this sort of narcissistic tailspin is not to stop hating yourself but to start hating someone else. There *are* people and ideas worthy of hatred, and there are few things that give an individual more dignity than to hate a formidable enemy. Yes, we need friends to love us and whom we can love without reserve; but we also need enemies to hate us and whom we can hate without reserve, without the moral constraints that stifle this natural and important emotion. Enemies, as the embodiments of our hatred, define us, give us shape, make us more pronounced; indeed, they force consciousness upon us so that we become sharply aware of values and constructs of character that the enemy threatens to destroy. When enemies come to mind or come into our presence, we do not go all mushy but stiffen and straighten up, taking on the bearing of an adversary in complete self-command, not necessarily righteous but certainly forceful.

Now, when I talk about enemies, I do not mean people whom you merely dislike, or merely dislike very, very much. Hatred is not to be devalued by lessening its object. There are people who annoy, who pester, who rub the wrong way. There are also the minor con artists in one's life, as well as those who are too dense to understand what you are about and why some things are vitally important to you. But these are not the people who inspire genuine hatred. The person you hate must embody a principle or value that is so abhorrent to you, so opposed to your sense of ethics and justice, that they inspire something very close to an urge to kill.

Ah, but here's the rub: I can only truly hate what I am capable of doing, or have done, myself. Nothing else can touch me deeply enough, can reach my own stygian, implacable self-hatred. I hate people with a profound and awesome hatred, for example, who betray my confidence. But I am capable of this hatred only because I have done my share of betraying. I not only hate them, I am entitled to hate them; and it is partly through cultivating my hatred that I build a dignity and respect for my own capability. By so respecting my capacity to do things I hate, I also build an inhibition to act them out. *Doing what my enemy does is not beyond my capacity, but beneath my dignity.* This recognition also preserves me from the self-righteous delusion that I am morally better than my enemy, and so I need neither dehumanize the enemy nor inflate myself with false virtue.

Hatred, as with any great passion, sooner or later has the power to call my reflective attention to itself, rather than to my literal enemy. It is my own hatred that engages me finally, not my enemy. This is an important, indeed critical, psychological move, for if at some point we cannot shift our vision from the external, literal enemy to an internal sense of some deep psychic necessity coming forth in this hateful attitude, then we are compelled to act out our hatred any way we can, through malicious gossip or a bullet through the enemy's brain.

While making important distinctions, we need to not get caught in false divisions: one needs the literal enemy in order to see the projection by reflection as it is mirrored back to you. As a dark form of Eros, hatred makes for relationship between the two of you, between outer and inner enemy, between objective and subjective enemy, between literal enemy and the psychic experience of enmity. Withdrawing projections from a literal enemy does not completely accomplish the psychological task, and does not necessarily mean you will then love them. On the contrary, their fuller reality may be even more hateworthy.

Hatred, just as much and in some ways more so than love, is a *via regia* through one's unconsciousness. It is a path to self-knowledge *par excellence*. The comic strip character Pogo said it well: "We have met the enemy and they are us." Show me what you hate and I will tell you what your character is made of, what your values are, and where your pathologies have their genesis. I can know who you are and what you stand for as much by what you hate as by whom you love.

Hatred arouses and energizes. An encounter with an enemy hardens the eyes, darkens their color, produces a flush of rage in the cheeks. There is an icy place in the heart's left ventricle. Lungs expand with oxygen, muscles tighten. Hatred turns one into an athlete.

But when hatred is completely exteriorized and thus still unconscious, hatred may also reduce us to silly, blithering idiots. It is not always a strong, energizing, noble passion. Consider how hatred is often initially a form of infatuation. The meaning of *infatuation* in Latin is "foolish," or "silly;" the infinitive *infatuare* means, simply, "to make a fool of." It is a state of possession in which one is not in customary control and may act like a fool. One may do something incredibly silly to avoid the enemy at a party, or say something unbelievably stupid. Have you ever found yourself in a large group of people and, across a crowded room, spotted a person you hate? It is an enchanted evening. (This happens to me on rare occasions. The climactic moment of joy comes when my enemy sees me – and leaves. Desertion on the field of battle, and I the victor.) If it is an important hatred, chances are very good that the rest of the meeting or party will be spent being acutely conscious of that person's presence. You may spend a lot of time trying to avoid them. You may try to introduce their name innocently into conversation, in the hope someone else might speak badly of them, or relay some gossip that can be stored for future ammunition. Perhaps you circulate around to be sure the enemy sees *you*, in an effort to cause him or her as much irritation as possible.

How is all this so different from the foolish antics of infatuated lovers? Instead of gazing into the beloved's eyes, one glares; instead of the beloved's name spoken with the flavor of honey and in a voice of silk, the enemy's name has the taste of metallic ash and texture of rusted iron; instead of listening to hear the beloved's virtues praised, one listens for proof of the enemy's despicable vices.

But once the reflective move is made, once your attention shifts from the literal enemy to the quality of hatred itself, you begin to regain the sense of your own power, and the stygian depth of your own psychological truth.

Hesiod the poet tells us that if dissension and strife break out amongst the immortals of Olympus, and if one of them takes refuge in a lie, then Zeus sends the messenger Iris to bring some of the icy water of Styx back in a golden bowl. Then the god or goddess must drink of the cup of hatred and risk the curse that accompanies perjury if they have spoken falsely. The taking of such an oath is a sacrament. And the effect of mighty Styx is quick and inevitable: if a god does indeed perjure himself, he is struck down unbreathing for a great year (which is nine regular years), and cannot talk, or eat, or drink. Then he is banished from the counsels of the gods for nine great years. Thus he is comatose, numb, inactive, in a waking death for eighty-one years as mortals reckon them.

Psychological perjury, put most simply, is lying about who you are, or not living according to your character. If one insists upon committing psychological perjury, one might as well be dead, for it has the effect of making one psychologically comatose, having vital signs but no vitality. And it is well to remember here that in a country whose national icon is a smiley face, and where it is thought more important to forgive enemies than to legislate serious gun control, that the price of lying about who we are or not speaking our full "truth" must be paid by our children. For the curse of our lies is carried by them, because "the sins of the fathers are visited upon the children to the third and fourth generation."[8]

The oath water of Styx, that sacred stuff of hatred, is cold and chill and unmoved by considerations of mercy, love, sympathy, or mitigating circumstances. For her, truth cannot be qualified. But such unyielding fixity is not necessarily symptomatic of psychopathic insanity; we should not hate hatred because it is insane, still less because it is inhuman. On the contrary, hatred, in its insistence on truth, preserves the clarity of reality, admits of no illusion or delusion. The clear water of Styx is unpolluted. And we should respect it precisely because it is inhuman, because it partakes of divinity, and therefore is not subject to all manner of deceits and lies and qualifications and the thousand natural equiv-ocations that flesh is heir to. It is not hatred itself that makes for disease or psychopathology; it is *perjury* that makes us sick.

The river Styx flows around the Underworld, girds it, binds it, confines it, and thus gives it ultimate definition. The image of Styx encircling the Underworld conveys the sense of limitation hatred places on our psychic lives, but also shows us where the outermost limit of tolerance *is*. Contrary to the image given by St. Paul, in *this* ancient image we are not constrained by love but by hatred. Our psychic lives and loves are encircled, bounded by, constrained by hatred. And the point is not to burst these bonds, break free and love more; no, the point is to honor that river, respect its depth, hold sacred that eternal limitation, and recognize how it gives greater sharpness and intensity to all the other qualities and experiences it encircles.

That hatred encircles the Underworld suggests that when we heroically push ourselves beyond our limits in pursuit of positive growth, when we go too far in a manic quest for peak experience, when we reach too far to grasp that elusive "human potential," we come up against the impassable Goddess Styx. The real harm of the human potential movement is that it has swelled our expectations to cosmic, titanic proportions. The potential of the human is imagined to span beyond infinity, all blessing, no curse, as if, with enough love, Styx would dry up and disappear, or as if enough good will and positive thinking will get her to miraculously part, like her cousin the Red Sea, so that we may walk through untouched, unscarred, unchanged, oblivious to the limits of human being.

In short, by refusing to see that we are confined by divine hatred, we refuse to see that we are confined at all. If change is wanted or needed, it must happen within the confines or at the limit, not beyond it on the other, greener side. In a happy humanism we expect so much of the human that nothing much happens; the human is always potential, never actual. And when it is actualized in the form of a Stalin or Hitler or Boston strangler or Minneapolis rapist, we deny it and say, "No, this is not human at all, this is inhuman – this is not what I meant."

But while hatred limits us in important ways, it also gives us shape, boundaries that secure us and give us security, marking perhaps the division between human being and the realm of the divine. Styx is hated, remember, because she requires and ensures *truth*. She does not require the best, or most noble, or most lovable, or most positive; only truth. And God knows how rare and complicated and elusive and hard to come by "truth" is, especially when we each live with many psychological truths, often contradictory. Styx does us the supreme service of guaranteeing, under penalty of deathlikeness, that we will be as true in our unspeakable horror as in our sweetest bliss. Styx guarantees that we remember the truth of Auschwitz as well as the truth of Christmas.

Notes

1. Ecclesiastes 3:1–2 (Revised Standard Version).
2. Jung describes the component of the psyche called the "shadow" as "the thing a person has no wish to be" (*CW* 16, para. 470), the sum of all those qualities, aspects, or characteristics that are considered unacceptable by the conscious ego-personality and which it seeks to hide.
3. I Corinthians 13:4–7, 8, 14:1.
4. Hesiod, *Theogony*, ll. 771–93, translated by Dorothea Wender, London: Penguin Books, 1973.
5. Shylock to Bassanio, friend of Antonio, *The Merchant of Venice*, Act I, Scene iii.
6. Richmond Lattimore, *Themes in Greek and Latin Epitaphs*, Urbana: University of Illinois Press, 1962, p. 115.
7. Ibid., p. 117.
8. Exodus 20:5.

Chapter 7

The archetype of the victim

> Cordelia: We are not the first who, with best meaning, have incurred the worst. For thee, oppressed king, I am cast down. . . .
>
> Lear: Upon such sacrifices, my Cordelia, the gods themselves throw incense.
>
> (Shakespeare, *King Lear*, Act V, scene iii.)

The archetypal figure of "the victim" is fraught with social connotations, religious associations, and psychological paradox, but I will limit my scope here to two aspects: the secular and the sacred. I will speak less of the psychosocial experience of literal victims than of the victim figure in the psyche, an archetypal image appearing in as many forms as there are woundings, injustices, and sacrifices.

We are all victims, though some of us, in whom the inner victim figure is denied or projected, may not be aware of a deeper psychic resonance in those critically important moments when suffering is inflicted. We all suffer, randomly, or by some seemingly inscrutable design. We all have far less power to control our sense of well-being in an increasingly chaotic world than we would like.

The archetypal victim image is a personification of how an individual or group imagines itself in its suffering. This is the "sacred victim," with its attendant associations of eternity and transcendence. The sacredness of the victim image refers primarily to its "set-apartness," its interiority as a psychic figure and its inner meaning.

By distinction, a criminal act upon a victim is a literal event which forces a condition of victimhood upon an individual or group, usually through violent means. The locus and temporality of this victimization makes it secular: it happens in the world, in the dimension of time. The distinction between the secular and the sacred, the "out there" and the "in here," does *not* make them mutually exclusive; to do so would split the archetype.

In our culture and time, the word *victim* evokes the negativity attached to the darkest and most painful experiences: suffering, injustice, powerlessness, and death. We almost always think of "victim" in its secular sense, perhaps because we have lost much of the sense of the sacred *in* the mundane, and feel only with difficulty (if at all) the deeper resonance of ancient claims of near-forgotten gods and goddesses being made upon us. Our world is largely and one-sidedly secular and we are confined in it. Having no other "world" to appeal to for help or justice, the victim in contemporary America is indeed a victim of the world of crime, homelessness, contagious disease, and drug madness.

The word *victim* evokes as well the terrible fear and insecurity of arbitrary randomness, or the equally terrible fear of having been singled out, "chosen," for unbearable pain. We use the word in connection only with those experiences we dread: cancer victim, rape victim, crash victim, victim of mental illness, victim of starvation. Whoever or whatever does the victimizing is important to the constellation of the victim experience, for it is these agents – cancer, rapist, car or plane – that create the context in which a person becomes a victim. Part of the horror of victimization is the realization that victim and victimizer share a terrible affinity: something in one may be found in the other. This does not mean they are simply two sides of the same coin; rather, both may be constellated in one person at one time. One may victimize oneself. To the victim, the agent of victimization has the power to inflict suffering and pain, to deny justice, to cause death. And since the victim is, by definition, powerless, the primal emotion that always accompanies victimization is fear.

Yet, just because it arouses such fear and complete negativity, it is possible that no other archetypal image so constellates the human psyche's need to make suffering meaningful as the figure of the victim. The first desperate cry of the victim is, "Why me?" The horror in that violent act which creates the victim cries out for some meaning in pain, some purpose in anguish; there can be no acceptance of, or coming to terms with, one's victimization without the psyche's constellation of the sacred victim. We may be able to endure much pain, far more than we ever deserve or think ourselves capable of enduring; but Jung was right when he said that human beings cannot tolerate a meaningless life.

Keeping these two aspects of the victim image together provides a way of imagining the victim which incorporates a multiplicity of meanings and emotions without denying the raw terror and despair that accompanies the psyche's constellation of the victim image. It may also be that the only way out of the senseless hell of secular victimization is through the purposeful hell of sacred victimization – a shift in perception that moves the victim from the despair of random happening to a sense of conscious purposefulness.

The secular victim

The New Age is not a favorable climate for victims; the New Age is for winners, not losers. The relatively unconscious "victimizer" in the American collective psyche seems to be increasingly hostile to victims; indeed, such hostility is probably producing more victims. One need only look at the rising numbers of victims of violent crime, child abuse, drugs, AIDS, environmental toxins, scams and -isms of all kinds.

The apparent antidote to victimhood is paranoia: trust no one, use deadbolt locks in your home, practice safe sex in your own bed, buckle up in your car, wear a hard hat and keep a cool head at work, know your rights when dealing with smooth-talking salespeople, police, and therapists. The assumption is that the more you protect yourself, the less likely you are to become a victim. The image of the victim has been devalued by the long-cherished American conviction that victims are merely losers who didn't try hard enough to win.

The image of the secular victim and the situations that create it turn negative attention toward the victim, usually in the form of blame. Since the meaning of victimhood cannot be divorced from the cultural value context in which it is experienced, the victim will always appear blame-worthy and at fault in a culture that most highly values dominance, conquest, power, competition – just the things needed to victimize.

The victim embodies those qualities that conflict with, threaten, or challenge that value system. The most obvious example of the previous century is the Nazi (mis)perception of the Jews as an "infectious" and powerful people who would poison the purity of Aryan society and take over the world. Projection happens everywhere, in everyone, collectively and individually. Secular victims are thus made by projection: those who support and maintain the culture's dominant values project their own fear of powerlessness, helplessness, weakness and vulnerability on to whom-ever can be victimized. And since our culture does not have an equitable distribution of power, there are more victims than perpetrators: victims are likely to be individually victimized as women, people of color, children, animals; or collectively as Blacks, Jews, Native Americans, lesbians and gays, old people, handicapped people, and so forth.

It is of course the victims who are blamed for whatever trouble befalls them. Since the victim sustains the effect, she or he must in some way be the cause. Perhaps the root of this odd situation lies in the old Christian idea that sin invites retribution, while goodness deserves blessing. In this view, the victim's suffering is understood as retribution by divine justice through human agency; where there is retribution, there must be sin. The idea is still alive and well, though cast now in secular terms: whatever the victim "gets" the victim "deserves." In New Age terms, the victim "created" his or her reality.

But we do not, in fact, always create our own suffering; to think otherwise is to assume a grandiose godlike capability to make awful things happen. For the sake of psychological maturity, we must be able to separate the dictum that we are each responsible for our actions from the assumption that victims are responsible for their own victimization. If we cannot make this differentiation, the victim then becomes a pathologized figure, neurotically and one-sidedly regarding the world as victimizer. We are then unconsciously identified with the victim, either introjecting the guilt or projecting the blame. The psychological task, however, is not necessarily to eliminate blame but to learn to place it where it properly belongs.

The victim's horror, shame, and powerlessness at the hands of a perpetrator, and the collective blame that reinforces these feelings makes the victim a figure of no value in a culture that despises weakness. But at the same time, it is precisely the horror and shame and powerlessness that evokes our sense of tragedy, empathy, outrage against injustice, and sometimes even love. We perceive the victim as that figure in each of us who is weak, who suffers, feels wrongly accused, and is powerless to command justice. It is perhaps because the victim figure embodies the paradox of bearing unbearable suffering that it is able to move us so deeply to compassion, empathy, grief, and love. Only a psychopath is impervious to the suffering and power of the victim, because the psychopath is untouched by the power of Eros to be in some relationship to pain.

It is the experience of the victim figure in our own psyche that makes us conscious of our human capacity for sacrifice.

The sacred victim

While most dictionaries define *victim* primarily as a person who suffers from an injurious or destructive action or agency, personal or impersonal, the older meaning of the word retains the sense of the original root:

"victim" as "sacrifice." The original meaning of the word *victim*, from the Latin word *victima*, means "sacrificial beast," and refers to any living creature that is killed and offered to a god or godlike power. The word *sacrifice* comes from the Latin word *sacer*, from which we derive the English word *sacred*, meaning that which is holy, set apart, "devoted for sacrifice," dedicated to a god or some religious purpose.

It is significant that *sacer* also means "forfeit," "accursed," and "criminal." The victim, then, may be both innocent and accursed at the same time. While this "accursedness" may not accurately describe the nature of a victimization, it often corresponds to the victim's feeling of being cursed, singled out for punishment. The victim image often appears in psychic life as "the accursed one," as in the scapegoat figure, the one singled out for the sins of the many – precisely because it is innocent and undeserving of its fate.

In his essay, "Cancer in Myth and Dream," Russell Lockhart notes the paradox in the word *victim*, having in its older Latin roots the meaning of "increase" and "growth."[1] (In Greek, the root of "victim" is *auxo*, meaning "increase" or "growth," and is one of the names of the Charities, *Auxo*, "the waxing.") The victim image thus unfolds as a complex weave of apparently contradictory meanings. It is an image simultaneously evoking collective emotions and ideas of fear, negativity, divine power, holiness, persecution, doubt, innocence, anguish, growth, sacrifice, condemnation. Thus the victim image may present itself in its secularity as ugly, fearful, and secretly despised, or the victim image may appear as sacred, beautiful, and desirable.

How the victim consciously perceives her/his suffering can give meaning to personal victimization: one is not only sacrificed but becomes capable of making, or enacting, a sacrifice. Victimization, then, is as much a condition of some meaningful relationship with a god as it is a condition of meaningless suffering.

The realms of the sacred and the secular are not mutually exclusive; the terms are merely devices to help us differentiate aspects of experience. The psychological task of the victim is to perceive them as joined, to make the secular sacred, to make a worthy sacrifice of one's suffering: to honor the wound, value the vulnerable, cultivate compassion for one's injured soul.

The person who perceives or feels him or herself as suffering *for* (not only *from*) a deity, a cause, a principle, or a beloved, experiences a different aspect of victimhood: the value of sacrifice. What redeems the suffering and anguish of the victim is not necessarily the cessation of suffering, but the experience of meaning in it. Simone Weil reminded us, "At every blow of fate, every pain, whether small or great, say to oneself, 'I am being worked on."[2] The *willingness* to sacrifice has long been regarded by some religious systems as a moral virtue, antithetical to the sin of selfishness. But my focus here is not on morality or virtue or selfishness, but rather on the *capacity* for sacrifice when the experience of victimization makes sacrifice psychologically necessary.

It goes against the grain of all our ideas of justice to place the burden of sacrifice on the victim; it smacks of victim-blaming. But it is precisely within one's capacity to offer sacrifice that one finds meaning: the victim who is able to make a sacrifice becomes psychologically active in her or his affliction, a participant in the holy work of making meaning out of incomprehensible chaos. Whether the sacrifice consists of one's naïvety, innocence, cherished ideal, or self-image, one's capacity to yield to a deeper necessity is tested in victimization.

The value and importance of the figure to whom the sacrifice is made, or on whose behalf it is offered, is paramount in the making of meaning, for an unworthy object demeans the one who sacrifices. The perpetrator of a violent crime is never worthy of the victim's sacrifice; he is merely a mindless agent of archetypal forces, enacting their impersonal cruelty. Neither he nor those godlike powers he serves are concerned with the individual fate of the victim. The victim must find a worthy altar in her or his own psyche on which to lay that which has been taken. Thus the victim "redeems" what has been lost not by revenge, but by a sense that some deeper purpose in life has been served. Choosing what has already happened and giving conscious assent, not consent, to the reality of one's victimization is the beginning of conscious sacrifice. On a collective level, the demand for sacrifice historically has been disproportionately placed upon women in ways that most men (and many women) do not regard as truly or worthily sacrificial. Perhaps because of this legacy and the ongoing reality of woman-as-victim, it is difficult for many women, as well as many men, to imagine that anything is to be gained by making or being a sacrifice for any reason. Self-sacrifice goes against both self-absorbed New Ageism (where it is now called "co-dependency") and some of the deepest and strongest currents of feminist thinking.

Yet, surely, there must be a place for sacrifice. Is there a place in life for the value of suffering or enduring pain for the sake of someone dearly loved, or for a cherished cause? What else can it mean to be "holy" or "set apart" or "dedicated" unless there is some person or idea worthy of such devotion? Of what value is all our strength and power if we cannot yield them up and submit them to a greater value? Are we so consciously determined not to be victims that we have become incapable of sacrifice? If we cannot or will not give up or yield anything, have no sense of deeper ethical claims upon us than our own small selves, we have lost not only a vital capacity to relate to one another, but a fundamental experience of being human. Because it entails irreparable loss, it seems a tragedy to become a victim under any circumstances. But it is an equally terrible tragedy to be unwilling to sacrifice, because this signifies an inability to love.

The need of the victim to find meaning in her or his victimization is not the same as finding a "reason" for it. There may be no "reason" why one particular person becomes the victim of a drunk driver at a particular time and place. The "reason" *why* one becomes a victim may be profoundly different from the meaning the victim takes from the experience. And because each victim comprehends her or his victimization differently, the discovery of meaning is always an individual experience.

The first cry of the victim is, "Why me?" Since there is rarely an answer, it may be that "Why *not* me?" is a more productive question. Victimization tends to make one visible: one has been "chosen" by a victimizer. But the experience of victimization makes aspects of the victim visible to herself or himself as well, and with the shocking emotional immediacy characteristic of genuine trauma. From whatever circumstance or agent, victimization reveals the victim's courage or lack of it, the victim's limited control over circumstance, the victim' depth of fear and shame, the victim's capacity for self-compassion, or the depth of the victim's self-recrimination.

Contained within the figure of the victim is a lesson concerning the nature of the god to whom sacrifice is being offered, for the victim bears the likeness of the god. The ancients believed there was a profound, though sometimes hidden, affinity between the sacrificial victim and the god to whom such offering was made. In Jewish tradition, the justice of God required a sacrificial animal to be innocent and well-formed; hence the lamb without blemish. The Christian myth requires that the sacrificed Son be like the sinless Father. In that region of the soul where we are victimized, through whatever circumstance, we must look for the likeness of a god, and there build an interior altar to ensure that our sacrifice is made holy. The wisdom to be discovered is not that "you brought it on yourself," but that it brought you to your Self.

How we treat the inner "sacred victim" is the measure of how we treat the "secular victim" in the world. If our response to the injured animal or abused child in a night dream is to banish it (by forgetting the dream or denying the disturbance) or blame it ("bad dream," "didn't make sense," "made me afraid so I hit it with a shovel"), our ruthlessness will enable us to banish out-there victims from sight, memory and responsibility, or else we will treat such victims with the unconscious contempt that appears as pity. Anything but real concern, real compassion, real love.

The psychological necessity is not that we save the inner victim from all hurt and pain, but that we learn to accept and care about it in its woundedness. This means a sacrifice of the "savior" role, consciously and voluntarily giving up our fantasies of total independence and self-sufficiency. We cannot save ourselves, and we are not sufficient unto ourselves. Only someone with a pathological compulsion for autonomy and do-it-yourselfism would argue this. But the temptation to save and heal the victim is very great, and perhaps nowhere is it felt more deeply than among psychologists and psychotherapists who work with victims and are expected to do just that.

For this is where we take our inner victim: to the doctor. We go with our victim-feelings as to a healer-god regularly (as to church), bringing sacrifices (as in fees), making confessions, feeling vulnerable and defenseless behind our mechanisms, feeling betrayed and enraged when our expectations (as in prayers) are not answered. We want rewards for humility, solutions to problems, recognition for hard efforts, safety always, and, most of all, we want the doctor to love us while it hurts, and then stop the pain. For some, being a victim becomes confused with a misunderstood need to stay in pain to ensure that the love will not stop. The doctor may become a victim too, especially when she or he has an unconscious affinity with the patient. In those areas, the healer falls victim to the wounded, the persona of professional capability collapsing under the weight of impossible demands and expectations. The torment of the patient becomes the doctor's own.

Some victim images have exceptional power to move us emotionally because they incorporate nearly all the most essential characteristics of the archetypal victim. The image of Jesus, broken and bloody on the cross, is a complete and singular example of the sacred victim figure, embodying holiness, innocence, unjust persecution and suffering, and voluntary sacrifice. As a collective example, the Jews historically have been forced to enact the victim role with such repetition that the very name of the people has become practically synonymous with "victim." Photographic images of skeletal death camp inmates have given us an austere visual definition of archetypal victimization, which is why Jews began referring to the Nazi genocide as a holocaust, literally a "burnt offering." Most recently, we have seen pictures of blind rabbits, gassed cats, and tuskless dead elephants – victimized animals who, though sentient beings, cannot willingly sacrifice themselves for humankind's benefit (and no doubt would not, if asked). These are images whose strength is derived from the innocence of the victim (Jesus), the magnitude of suffering (the Holocaust), and the utter helplessness of the victim's condition (animals). Then, if Eros is awakened and illuminated by Psyche's lamp, these powerful images may call us into relationship with them and evoke our compassion and love.

As noted earlier, the root of the word *victim* carries an ancient meaning of "increase" or "growth." However, I am not suggesting that victimization ought to be considered an occasion of "positive growth." To do so minimizes the horror and fear and shame or represses them completely. The injunction to the victim to "grow" through adversity is a subtle appeal to the victim's ego to leave the victimization experience behind (a form of denial). "Growth" in this usage is defensive, the demand of an anxious parent who does not know what to do for a child in pain (as in, "Grow up, stop crying, stop feeling sorry for yourself").

A deeper objection to the demand on the victim to "grow" is that it keeps the experience of the victim within a fantasy of the child. Whatever complex meanings victimhood may have for the soul are obscured and reduced to false simplicity by forcing them into the single perspective of the child archetype. Thus the victim appears passively childlike or irresponsibly childish. This may be one reason why our culture takes a profoundly ambivalent attitude toward victims: either total neglect and abuse or idealization and galvanic convulsions to rescue. (Remember little Jessica McClure, who fell down a well in Texas in 1989? The whole country vicariously participated in the rescue operation.) When perceived through the child archetype, the victim is infantilized: whatever injury has been done can now only be understood as a sign or consequence of psychological immaturity – the naïvety of a child, the innocence of a child, the carelessness of a child, the abuse of a child, the child who cries for grownups to play fair. Instead of an adult drama deep in the soul's sacred interior, victimization is seen as one of many misfortunes that befalls a child. We demand either excessive responsibility of the victim ("She should have known better") or expect him or her to be as helpless in trauma as a child.

The victim figure needs rescue not from victimization but from the child fantasy. The idea of "increase" in the root of the word refers to something other than developmental "growth." What happens to us happens, avoidably or not; what we do psychologically with those happenings is what makes for "increase" or decrease. Russell Lockhart writes:

The psychology of . . . unwilling sacrifice is quite different from that of the willing sacrifice. There are moments and seasons in one's life when genuine sacrifice of the most valued thing is essential for further growth. If this sacrifice is not made willingly, that is, consciously and with full conscious suffering of the loss, the sacrifice will occur unconsciously. One then will not sacrifice to growth but be sacrificed to growth gone wrong.[3]

When the inner victim figure is thrown to the lion of the great goddess Necessity (*Ananke*), it is in that arena – wherever we are torn to pieces by pain or injustice – where blind Necessity must be turned into purposeful Fate. The events and experiences that bring us to pain, loss, grief, injury, and abandonment are the rites of passage and sacrificial offerings that "increase" us, that force maturation upon us.

The victim figure within us, wounded and helpless, is sometimes rescued by interior reflection, when the interior victimizer is also acknowledged. We may be victimized by any of our own thoughtless follies, character flaws, failures of foresight, errors of judgment, or self-betrayals. We may fall victim to any deity or archetypal power whose service we have neglected: Eros taunts us with insatiable desire, Saturn holds our joy and freedom hostage in his prison of depression, Hera drives us mad for monogamy, Aphrodite tortures us with jealousy and the insecurity of love.

But the interior victim is not always to be rescued: indeed, once rescued, it is no longer truly a "victim." That suffering, powerless figure within derives its meaning precisely from its suffering and powerlessness: it is this acceptance of human limitation and woundedness that is offered up as sacrifice to the powers, deities, gods, or archetypes that rule psychic life. It may be that the archetype of the victim, with its infinite loneliness in pain, is that image which holds the deepest knowing ("gnosis") of what it is to be "human." To know the "sacred victim" in oneself is that experience of the fatefulness and finitude of life that makes submission to one's humanity possible, sacrificing the very human desire to be god in all things.

Notes

1. Russell Lockhart, *Words as Eggs: Psyche in Language and Clinic*, Dallas: Spring Publications, 1983, p. 56.
2. Simone Weil, *Notebooks*, New York: G.P. Putnam's Sons, 1956, p. 266.
3. Lockhart, op. cit., pp. 57–8.

Chapter 8

Homo/aesthetics, or, romancing the self
for A.D.

'Beauty is truth, truth beauty,' – that is all
Ye know on earth, and all ye need to know.
(John Keats, *Ode on a Grecian Urn*)

Without warning
as a whirlwind
swoops on an oak
love shakes my heart.
(Sappho)

This is a musing, personal and subjective, about love and affinities. I have no inclination to theorize about love. I am an unabashed, anachronistic romantic, reconstructed, it is true, but a romantic nonetheless. And I am a near-insatiable sensualist, constantly craving smooth milky chocolate and blue moonlight, even though I wear the persona of a near-ascetic. While my mind reads books and takes in important data and thinks, it is my fingers, my hands, my mouth, my eyes, my skin that tell me pleasure and speak to me in the language of beauty. The language of beauty that speaks the truth of love is sensate and immediate, conveyed in touch and gesture. All ye need to know.

It has always felt to me rather chilling that Jungian psychology tends to speak of romantic love in terms of "projection,"[1] as if the *concept* of projection fully explained all we need to know about what makes the passion, the excitation, the depth and bittersweetness of erotic matings. Projection is, indeed, an inevitable mechanism and invaluable for consciousness; but to speak psychologically and aesthetically of love in such conceptual language reduces experience to concept, the organic thus rendered mechanical, psyche as machine. Conceptual explanatory language gives primacy to "mental insight" and assigns "bodily knowing" to second place, body as reactor to insight rather than as first discoverer of "truth." No mere mind-spawned word can leave such a taste of eloquence and knowledge on my tongue as can the soft skin of my lover's body. To imagine love in conceptual terms, however accurate the terms, is to separate love from body, to separate the beautiful from the sensate.

And then, Jungian psychology tends to speak almost exclusively of romantic love as *heterosexual* projection, not noticing that the thick emotionality and convolutions of the heart that attend romantic love are not at all different when the "other" is of the same sex. Women and men learn to interpret the eroticized aspect of animus or anima (unconscious masculine or feminine components in the psyche), projected on to a literal opposite-sex person, as romantic love. Not only do we so learn to interpret, we learn to *experience* this projection in a culturally predetermined way: finding beauty in what is not like ourselves because we have learned that that is where beauty resides, finding our sexual desire flowing out toward a figure we recognize as Other because we have learned that the "other" must be literally so, finding psychological reassurance in the normalcy of our sexual desire for literal otherness, because we have learned that this is the only real kind of love there is.

I remember, at sixteen, having a crush on the captain of the football team. It was 1958, and no doubt my as-yet-unrecognized lesbian self sought safety in convention. To this day, I do not know for certain how much of that crush was genuine, and how much of it I cultivated so that I could have the kind of heterosexual adolescence I was supposed to. But at sixteen, for certain, what made my blood rush was the lovely, enviable luster of my best friend's long black hair. During the day I thought about the football captain, but at night, alone in my bed, my fingers kneaded the air, like a cat's, wanting to touch her breasts. For the sake of normalcy, which to me meant survival, this truth I could not, would not, know.

The dictum that "opposites attract" has been narrowed to mean that only opposites can or do attract, as if the opposition of "otherness" is somehow more compelling and numinous than the attraction of "likeness." So what happens when the attraction – sexual, erotic, emotional, physical, mental, spiritual – is not to an "opposite" but to a "like?" What does it suggest that the phallic form, in my beholding eye, is a passionless aesthetic, interesting, but hardly compelling? How am I, as a woman, to understand overwhelming and wordless numinosity when it comes to me in the form and flesh of a woman like myself?

My male analyst in Zurich in the early 1970s once commented to me that my experience of "the numinous" always seemed to come through a woman. I was immediately struck by the emotional accuracy of his observation. Yes, it was so, had always been so. He had named my feeling, and thus I gained something important: an almost tactile piece of self-knowledge that began to take shape out of the vague emotions of nameless longing and bittersweetness that since childhood had floated uneasily around a veiled female psychic figure. However, we never fully pursued the implications of this truth to see what it would reveal of my deeper sexual self, a more authentic self than the one that was, at the time, having a mad and maddening affair with a black-eyed, handsome, wildly romantic stud.

We avoided following, or benignly neglected, the path of that particular truth: I no doubt because I was very afraid, didn't want to know, and the time for me to know was not yet; my analyst perhaps for the same reasons, or because it simply did not occur to him that there was something more to pursue. Now, nearly twenty years later, our "reasons" are irrelevant. What is important is that the essential piece of self-knowledge, the realization that "woman" is the carrier of the numinous for me, has been deepened, from mental insight to psychological reflection to knowledge embedded in the very flesh of my body. This began to happen when I was past forty years old, and so I had to go back to the beginning and start "knowing" all over again, in a different way, from a different source, through a different medium.

The different "way" is my body, the different "source" is my lesbian, rather than heterosexual, self, and the different "medium" is my female lover and mate. Of course, she and I project all kinds of things grandly, wildly, and sometimes painfully on to each other. But we are neither sexually opposite nor in sexual opposition, not agents or representatives of that realm of "the unknown." She is an "other" to me because she is different from me, but she is not my opposite. At first glance, many of our attitudes and approaches to life appear almost identical, informed by the fact and consciousness of our femaleness; yet our differences (not necessarily oppositional) can be dramatic. We are both introverted; but while she engages the world vigorously in corporate boardrooms, I flee to the seclusion of my study. We both want to be scholars and are academically minded; but the land and a farm are her deepest joys, while I dream of libraries and shelf-filled reams of paper. She wants dog and cat; I am content with cat. She is more maternal with children; I am maternal with her. Our endless making of differences from the same essences requires attention to detail, an ear for nuance, a love of subtlety. When we fail in these, we blur and lose ourselves for the time.

The individuation process requires that we become skilled in differentiation. In female/male romantic relationships, where the attraction of the opposite sex is attractive primarily because it is opposite, initial differentiation is relatively broad-brush. Our culture, and Jungian psychology to the extent that it serves the culture, makes such differentiation fairly easy, by defining for us what is female and what is male, and by pre-differentiating certain psychic components as abstract principles: "feminine" and "masculine."

A woman whom I love is "like myself" and "like my Self," requiring a differentiation now of the most minute, the most subtle separations of the smallest particulate matter(s), full of nuance. In this subtle likeness there are no broad categories of gender and sex into which to sort and contrast all the ways in which we are different, for in these ways we are not so different – and this is where we are as likely to be afflicted with psychic blindness as blessed with the most acute and penetrating vision. Because of our fundamental female likeness, the individuation process requires the most exact differentiation of the myriad shades of nuance that distinguish our projections. Projections on to a screen must become carefully noticed reflections into a mirror. She turns this way, I turn that. My individuation depends on being able to tell the difference between my projection (*what* I see of myself in her) and reflection (*how* I see my Self in her).

A heterosexual woman or man suffers a loss of soul by not knowing that figure in the psyche that delights in a homoerotic aesthetic. No one is one-sidedly sexually oriented, except those neurotic souls who are completely identified with one sexual polarity or another. The virulent heterosexual, whose homophobic fear of the inner self-lover may appear as Macho Man or Vacant Female, lives at one pole, while at the other pole lives the insistent homosexual, whose heterophobic fear of otherness in her/his own psyche may appear as self-limiting political correctness or thinly disguised contempt for the opposite sex. Total identification is especially psychologically limiting for heterosexuals because it is defined and accepted as "normal." They are encouraged, even threatened, to remain unconscious of that imaginal psychic figure within them who appreciates the beauty of sameness and is attracted to a sexual likeness.

By remaining unconscious of the homo/sexual aspect of themselves, exclusively heterosexually identified people leave a potentially creative and loving aspect of themselves split off from consciousness. If the self-lover within is banished to the darkest cavern of repressed fears, then a pathway of differentiation for the sake of individuation, marked by an appreciation of the subtle beauty of affinities, reaches a dead end. The same-sex-loving figure is forbidden to enter consciousness. Without loving one's self-lover, can one truly be a whole lover to anyone, being split at the root?

I believe there are some women whose interior image of the Self, of woman-as-goddess, woman-as-eminently-worthy-of-love, an image correlated with individual self-respect, suffers and deteriorates when that image is not embodied in a romantic sexual relationship with another woman. Romance, after all, is an aesthetic of the erotic imagination, a *fabula*, to use one of the Latin words for "romance," or the fabulous telling of a love story. Because romance celebrates Eros as "first-born and fairest of the gods," romance is one of the ways we worship, and making love is the making of prayer.

I think women, as "idea," are beautiful. I think my woman lover, as a person, is beautiful. The beauty I see reflected back to me from the mirror of my lover's soul is my own, and she sees her own in me. The divine presence of Eros attends such psychic reflection in the form of physical passion. To be able to recognize this beauty as my own soul is more a redeeming truth than a pathological form of narcissism, which is, sadly, the only way we have been taught or allowed to "know" this reflection.

The terrible anguish of Narcissus, who cannot touch the face of his own soul, is a psychologically instructive story of projection that cannot be claimed, a lesson about how one's soul may be lost and one's life with it. But the romance in the myth of Narcissus has been severely pathologized, defined in modern terms and times as a personality disorder, as if the appreciation of the beauty of one's image and the longing for a soulmate of one's own and in one's own likeness, are symptomatic of disorder. The conventional warnings against narcissistic introspective indulgence are, as Murray Stein wrote, evidence for the deeper knowledge of how strong the "reflective instinct" is, that there exists in psyche a "powerful tendency in the direction of Narcissus," and that one "has a profound unconscious love of [her] own soul and of the activity of reflecting upon [herself] for [her] own pleasure." The taboo against self-absorption is intended to protect us from the "fascination and beauty" of one's soul-image.[2]

An equally strident disapproval of the narcissian way of loving comes through our culture's pervasive and deeply rooted homophobia, the collective dread of self-attentiveness that looks reflectively within and finds one's own image to be stunningly beautiful and desirable.

The psychic image of Narcissus, gazing into the pool with desire and lovesick eyes, does not want an explanation of itself, it wants itself. That sweet, beautiful youth of not-yet-fixed gender is itself an image of wanting, and of wanting denied.

. . . he saw
An image in the pool, and fell in love
With that unbodied hope. . . .

Everything attracts him
That makes him so attractive. Foolish boy,
He wants himself; the loved becomes the lover
The seeker sought, the kindler burns.[3]

Beautiful, young, and indeterminate, Narcissus is an image of undifferentiated eroticism, knowing only itself and not an "other." Anyone who remains poolside with Narcissus suffers his fate. For one brief moment, though, where perhaps we all begin, in that eternal moment of gazing into one's reflection – just before one reaches for the untouchable, before one begins to waste away with impossible love and unmet desire – in that moment, one may perceive one's beauty as one's true self, and one's truth as a beautiful self. At this moment, the love of affinities, the romantic longing to touch and embrace and caress one's likeness, is born. Even after one leaves the pool's water-mirror, the image remains in one's psyche always, an icon, a thing of beauty that endures forever. But now the beholder must move on and find an "other" who can best embody that image now engraved in the soul, an "other" whose living heart beats with the same rhythm.

No one myth is adequate for a whole human life. The tale of Narcissus is a tragedy in one act. One's life needs at least a second act, conscious action, to move the individuation process to a romantic, satisfying, as close to happy ending as possible. Reflection is not enough. Psyche needs erotic embodiment. Not enough is the distant coolness of fixed image, however lovely. The body wants wetness and heat and throbbing of blood, impact of muscle, particular scent.

Narcissism is a pathology not when it suggests homosexuality, but when it excludes love of an Other, an Other of either sex whose separate reality ought to evoke and excite love rather than preclude it. The merely-gazing and mournful self-absorption of pathological narcissism do not belong to an aesthetic of romantic same-sex love, yet the aesthetic of such love is created in the narcissistic passion to embrace one's essential self in its unique, separate beauty. Put another way, the aesthetic of same-sex romantic love requires not only a narcissistic passion for one's own image, but also a differentiated eroticism that recognizes in an "other" a worthy self-likeness. My love is not only of self; it is requited in the image of my lover's face, and all my senses, feasting on her, draw forth my delighted recognition.

Women who love women sexually have long been accused of (among other things) psychological infantilism, of wanting to regress to the womb, to merge mindlessly with the Mother. (Odd, how little this "pathology" has been theoretically differentiated from the presumed psychology of gay men.) Lesbian sexuality has been seen as childish and immature. Some theorists still judge such sexuality as a "phase" to be outgrown, appropriate only to adolescence. Too many heterosexual men still think that all a lesbian – of any age – needs to help her "grow up" is "a real man." This is as absurd as assuming that the reason women love men sexually is because they hate their mothers and are trying to become men by sexual assimilation.

How ungenerous such disembodied theorizing is to a soul in love. Such bald ideas have no truth in them for me because they are not beautiful, have no substance, no body with skin and fine animal fur, are not congruent with what my flesh knows as intimate fact (her rose-petaled lips, the line of her throat, the exquisite symmetry of her eyelashes).

What first captures the heart and desire of Narcissus is beauty, his reflected beauty. There is health in falling in love with another of the same sex who embodies one's own form, in finding it beautiful, even in identifying with it – as in, "this lovely woman, this too is me, for I also am a woman." Homo/sexuality, or sexuality among sames, is a recognition of homo/aesthetics and can be affirmed on grounds of beauty, as well as and apart from any other.

Mnemosyne is the Mother of the Muses, whose name means Memory. She is the matrix of all art, poetry, and song, and the Greeks correctly perceived that history, too, is an art. Without Mnemosyne, I could not remember myself as a woman; but when I recall my first, original, archetypal female form, when I recall the tender and wild Beauty that attends all Love in her first form, then Memory sends a daughter to me, and my Lady Muse leads me back to the memory of beauty and first love. Audre Lorde wrote in a love story, " . . . wherever I touched, felt right and completing, as if I had been born to make love to this woman, and was remembering her body rather than learning it deeply for the first time."[4]

So it is true, after all, what those theorists say: "lesbianism" is a way of returning to the womb, but there is a vast difference between "regression" and "return." The desire to return to one's source – an archetypal desire, not a particularly homosexual one – can be construed as "regression" only in a culture like ours, which fears the Mother and elevates the Father as a defense against her. For women, return to the Mother is not necessarily regression; it is a return to whatever form of woman we are intended to become.

There is more going on in lesbian loving than we know. Somewhere far below the cultural accretions, the social prohibitions, the legal obstacles, the psychological confusions, the developmental mistakes, and the religious judgments – somewhere my self is seeking a Self, its own original maternal image writ large, and as naturally as sunrise the numinous Self comes to me through a woman and in her form. To feel myself returning to this Mother-Self is like coming home. My body remembers that home; my body is that home, re-created.

The power of Mnemosyne, Mother Memory, is felt in the body. The mother of all art quickens the sensual body, recalling me to remember what has been lost as I have grown up and away from the Mother: self-knowledge, self-love, self-respect, self-pleasure. This is too much loss. The Patriarch is relentless in his destruction of perceived female threats to his high place. He has tried to make the world an arid, cold, dangerous place, as unlike the womb as he can imagine.

If I follow my Muse, she can restore these losses, through whatever art she gives me to embody, as a way of recreating my first home, my deepest self. My Muse, like my lover, guides my sensate touch to an enduring mystery in my Self. Indeed, she takes me to herself, her own temple. When the Muse is upon me, caressing and arousing me, my body's memory recalls and calls forth yet again all the deep pleasures I have known of woman. Then once more, like a whirlwind, "love shakes my heart."

Notes

1. The literal meaning of "projection" is to "throw forth," and is used in psychology to refer to the mechanism by which qualities and contents within an individual are projected on to another person, so that one's internal reality is seen as an external reality of the other. This is not a conscious act, and so it is sometimes difficult to see that what has been "thrown forth" really belongs to one's own personality.
2. Murray Stein, "Narcissus," in *Spring: Archetypal Psychology and Jungian Thought*, New York: The Analytical Psychology Club of New York 1976, p. 39.
3. Ovid, *Metamorphoses*, Rolfe Humphries (trans.), Bloomington: Indiana University Press, p. 70, ll. 419–22 and 429–32.
4. Audre Lorde, "Zami: A New Spelling of My Name," Freedom, California: The Crossing Press, quoted in Laura Chester (ed.), *Deep Down: The New Sensual Writing by Women*, Boston: Faber and Faber, 1989, p. 237.

Chapter 9

Sexual encounters of the third kind

The whole world is interested in sex. Americans are practically obsessed with it. But as an interest in sex conflicts with traditional Christian strictures against the "wrong" kinds of sex, the word "sexuality" has gained currency to signify what we all know: there is more to sex than just sex.

Psychology, beginning in the mid-nineteenth century, has been very interested in sex of all kinds. In 1886, the Austrian psychiatrist Richard von Krafft-Ebing published a compendium, *Psychopathia Sexualis*, including 238 cases of every sexual anomaly one could imagine, and several one could not. Krafft-Ebing began the book with a florid, romantic introduction extolling the virtues of Christendom above all other religions, especially "Islamism," and exalting Woman as the purest ideal of asexual humanity.

> Above all things Islamism excludes woman from public life and enterprise, and stifles her intellectual and moral advancement. The Mohammedan woman is simply a means for sensual gratification and the propagation of the species; whilst in the sunny balm of Christian doctrine, blossom forth her divine virtues and her qualities of housewife, companion and mother. What a contrast![1]

Krafft-Ebing waxes orgasmic for several following pages. He is more enthralled with sex than Freud, who was more enthralled with sex than Jung. Fortunately for psychology and culture, both Krafft-Ebing and Freud made enormous contributions, theoretically and clinically, to our understanding of human sexual life. Jung went in another direction: his unique contribution was to help us see the spiritual dimension of sex, particularly through his conception of archetypes, rescuing it from psychology's reductionistic interpretations.

The problem with Jung is subtle. His ideas of sex are separate from the body in a way that Krafft-Ebing's and Freud's are not; it might not be inaccurate to say that his ideas about sex are disembodied, and can be best understood through the spirit. His thinking about sexuality was, in a sense, subversive to the psychology of his time, and certainly so in a Christian culture which had always exalted the spirit and lamented the body as gross matter, source of sin and illness.

As usual, however, there is more than meets the eye. Jung's ideas appear to be not so obviously far removed from the reality and experience of women, as were Freud's, and his psychology is not so overtly rooted in the superiority of Christianity, as was Krafft-Ebing's. But just because of the covert assumptions in Jung's theory, we need to turn a penetrating, even suspicious, eye on it. Like the subject of sex itself, Jung's theory of archetypal sexual psychic figures (particularly the "contrasexual" figures of *anima* and *animus*) needs to be subverted, because if we don't see more deeply into it, we will be led off into the spirit realm and leave behind the immediate, sensate body where sex actually happens and where theory – if it is good theory – is lived.

It is still hard to find Jungians of the third and fourth generation who talk and write about sex in its own terms and not just in terms of the spirit or archetypal significances. But sexual encounters of any kind mean just that: a close encounter with someone or something that is sexual, as in sex of the rutting around variety, the crashing of one lust against another, of hot bodies and secretions and juices and countless erogenous zones, not to mention all those mind-blowing physical sensations that exhaust our capacity to find adequate metaphors: skin soft as silk, taste sweeter than chocolate, lips like honey or wine, flesh firm or yielding, insistent, wet, strong, dark, surging, and on and on and on. Read any Gothic romance or D.H. Lawrence or parts of the Kenneth Starr Report and you get the point, but you probably get it better when you fling yourself with abandon into a wildly sensual, sexual moment.

I began imagining sexual encounters of at least three kinds when I discovered that there is an actual institution of the Federal Government called the Center for Unidentified Flying Objects, which recognizes three kinds of encounters with UFOs. These can be read metaphorically as three modes of sex. A close encounter of the *first kind* refers to a UFO seen at close range but which does not interact with the environment. This might be imagined as a casual sexual encounter, a sort of quick, of-the-moment, historically frequent male approach to sex. Close encounters of the *second kind* are those in which a UFO interacts with the environment and has a physical effect on plants, trees, animals, and humans. I read this as a somewhat more complex sexual encounter, having more than casual import, and a historically usual female approach to sex. A close encounter of the *third kind* is that in which alien beings are reported to be in or near a UFO and abductions of humans occur. (I find it very odd that the Center for UFOs does not consider that humans might want *voluntarily* to depart with alien beings.) This is the kind of close encounter you read about in the shocker tabloids or see in science fiction movies. So a sexual encounter of the third kind involves being "taken" by something "alien," something as yet unconsidered, a new image of sexual and erotic engagement.

Sexiness and eroticism, like beauty, are in the eye of the beholder. We need to twist the lens a bit and develop a "sexual eye," a way of seeing that which is not usually imagined as sexy or erotic as in some way being so, because this is one of the ways in which the physical world becomes animated, beautiful, attractive. Even computers can be erotically alluring: they have floppy disks, they have hard drives, and they need surge protectors. My computer enjoys S/M games: he likes to boot up and tell me "Bad command!"

Before we know what any sexual encounter "means," symbolically, spiritually, intrapsychically or interpersonally, our *bodies* know what it means. But if we don't know how to listen to our bodies, we think only minds have something to say. In fact, we think bodies are something we have rather than something we are. We say, "I *have* a body" instead of "I *am* body:" the body conceived in terms of ownership rather than as essence or experience. I have discussed this human perceptual aberration with my three cats, and they, completely intact and seamless creatures that they are, look at me with pity and walk away to find the nearest patch of sunlight for a serious nap. With this gesture they want to remind me that my habitual Jungian talk about "symbols" and "spirituality" and "transcendent function" is all well and good, but the most important things, the ultimate values, the true metaphysical realities of life, are to be found in two simple things: a perfect patch of sunlight in which to warm your erogenous fur, and the deep pleasures of a roll in the catnip.

Sexual encounters of the third kind are exciting because the third kind of *anything* is exciting. Our thinking and images, especially thinking and images of gender, are in twos: male/female, masculine/feminine, couples and couplings, two-parent families. The third kind of something suggests a mystery, or something bizarre, or something transcendent, as Jung puts it, that lifts us out of the conflict between opposites.

And the third kind of anything, especially in the areas of gender and sexuality, is exciting, and sometimes frightening, because it signifies the entry of a new attitude, a shift of perception and thinking and feeling to allow what before had been alien.

The movement in the last several years toward cultural diversity in all spheres of American life has not fully included sexual diversity as part of the way we imagine an enriched psychical and cultural life. For example, even though there is greater social and political recognition of homosexuality – although not without a recent growing backlash – the national consciousness does not regard homosexuality as a fully valid and equally valued sexual orientation.

Different sexualities, like alien beings from UFOs, are still frequently regarded as disruptive rather than merely diverse. Most people who come to psychotherapy with gender and/or sexual problems are afflicted in this way because these are the problems in our culture. They are not mere personalisms. Our culture is burdened with all sorts of "gender identity disorders" (a diagnostic category in psychiatry's *Diagnostic and Statistical Manual*) and with all kinds of sexual worries, fears, and hurts.

Psychology – certainly depth psychology – should be more subversively concerned with changing the culture than with changing the patient, because what the patient needs – any patient, any of us – is not to learn how to adapt to the *status quo*, but how to change the *status quo* so it won't make us sick. Nowhere in modern American life is this more apparent and pressing than in the collective *status quo* that regulates our attitudes about gender and sexuality.

Since the usual construct of sexuality requires us to think of sex in terms of male and female – categories which come loaded with countless associations and expectations of what male and female *are*, or *should be* – I am imagining a close encounter of the third kind as a perspective of sexual life conceived in non-gendered terms: sexuality that is neither primarily male nor female, neither essentially masculine nor feminine, that is not predetermined by one's anatomy or socially constructed gender role.

A third kind of encounter is with an alien part of the sexual imagination, from the outer edge of inner space, from beyond the pale of our customary conceptions of the sexually normal and ordinary. I am imagining an encounter with varieties of sexualities in which the improbable meets the expected and makes a new, third kind of reality.

There are three problems to be addressed here. First is the problem of genderism and its offshoot, sexism. Most of Jung's psychology, as with most other psychologies, rests on inaccurate assumptions about gender and the relationship between gender and sexuality. Second is the problem of over-spiritualization of sex in Jungian tradition. This has been, in part, a necessary compensation to an overly reductive, materialistic, biological view of sexuality in psychology for about 150 years. But the Jungian tendency has been to leave the body and go on spiritual quests instead. (This is like a close encounter of the first kind: not much interaction with the physical environment.)

The third problem is with Jung's "animus" concept, which is one of the cornerstones of his theory about the structure of the female psyche, and which is built on those same assumptions of gender and sexism referred to in the first problem. For Jung, the "animus," briefly defined, is an archetypal image in a woman of her unconscious, masculine side, and is the factor that makes all sorts of qualitative projections about spirit, intellect, creativity, and not least, sexual attraction or repulsion. But the animus, as Jung conceived it in stereotypical genderized terms, is a limited and often false portrayal of female sexuality, and keeps us all, women and men both, locked into the confines of unconscious genderism and a one-sided definition of "normal."

It is practically impossible to say anything about sex without saying something about gender. In our culture they are so confused and undifferentiated as to be synonymous. Considering the fact that they have *been* confused for about 5,000 years, it is no small effort to try to separate them. I believe that one of the major tasks of our species is to begin to differentiate and separate ideas of *gender* from ideas of *sex*. This means reimagining both from the ground up, discarding old concretized conceptual structures into which we have locked gender definitions and roles, and realizing that we have been cramming all human sexual possibilities into a tiny little psychic space no bigger than a condom.

The problems of gender we deal with today, in the spheres of religion, politics, and psychology, are not just the apparent questions of whether women and homosexuals should be ordained to ministry, or under what conditions gays should be allowed in the military, or whether women or gay men should be Boy Scout troop leaders. The real problem underlying all these questions is that we don't know how to think about gender and sexuality in any terms other than heterosexuality, and a sexist heterosexuality at that.

Consider how subtly and subliminally genderism and heterosexism influence the tone of public political debate. I am thinking beyond the protracted absurdities we endured from Congressional voyeurs pumping away at the Clinton mess. There is very little subtlety or subliminality here, but quite a lot of unconsciousness and silly posturing. For a more interesting and less obvious example, think back with me to the early days of the Clinton administration. When President Clinton nominated the first woman for the post of U.S. Attorney General, Zoe Baird, the questions at the Senate confirmation hearings were based – at least partly – on collective assumptions about the role and responsibilities of women, and particularly mothers. There were alleged improprieties about the legality of daycare for their children and payments for it by the nominee. Baird was not confirmed. Kimba Wood, the second nominee, ran into the same problem, and also was not confirmed.

The person who finally got the job was a six-foot-tall woman with no husband and no children. These were the first three characteristics by which Janet Reno was introduced to the public, repeated like a litany for days after her nomination as if to make sure we all understood that these were the *most important* things we needed to know about her. So we could think of her then as more neuter than female, or more like a man because she isn't much like most other women, and a lot less like the two attractive but morally deficient female nominees who preceeded her.

As a society, we have not deeply questioned gender roles – at least, not in a way that really welcomes answers. We haven't truly examined our most fundamental assumptions about gender, and roles, and sexuality – which tells us that these are the areas in which we are most severely repressed. In our culture, *sex* is the great repressed, and as Freud correctly observed, the repressed always returns. And therefore, sex is everywhere, and always troublesome, since when the repressed returns, it returns in the form of a symptom. These days, when we deal with matters of sex, we deal with sex not as a genuine matter, an alchemical *prima materia* full of riches and possibilities, but as a symptom, a carrier of disease or badge of perversion, cause of unwanted pregnancy, subject of dispute in every area of public and private life, from sex education in schools to the annual *Sports Illustrated* swimsuit edition, cause of some of our worst shame and violent crimes, from sexual abuse of children to secret fantasies of sadomasochism, from personal worries about private sexual impotence to public debates about sex as a form of political power.

Our assumptions about gender and sexuality are rooted in ancient, unconscious notions about women, men, reproduction, and sexual pleasure, all of which long ago were cast in the form of *theological* ideas, increasingly encrusted over time with more and more notions, eventually taking on the character of dogma (implicit, if not stated). The Christian schema of gender – God on top, men in the middle, women at the bottom – is still the schema that dominates the collective psyche. The Western psyche, so strongly influenced by the monotheistic religions of Judaism, Christianity, and Islam, still imagines gender in terms of their tenets of hierarchy and predetermined roles; their assumptions of God-given characteristics of each gender; their ways of valuing some characteristics over others; and especially the moral tone that underlies all thinking about gender roles, and about sexuality and its expressions. It is no accident, for example, that all modern objections to human homosexuality are based on religious and moral beliefs, not scientific knowledge. (And there are a lot of Jerry Falwells and Pat Robertsons who think that homosexual behavior amongst *animals* is immoral too.)

When psychology began to emerge as a separate field of study in the mid-nineteenth century, it took over religion's assumptions about gender and sexuality and secularized them. Instead of talking about the law of God, it talked about the law of Nature. Instead of talking about the God-given role of women, it talked about the natural biological functions of women. Instead of citing the biblical injunction to "be fruitful and multiply," psychologists – all males – announced that the "natural" function of healthy-minded women is to be mothers. This "truth" could not be doubted because, first, it was announced by men who spoke with the authority that was God-given to their gender, and secondly, it was clearly scientific because it was an unchanging and clearly observable fact that women, and not men, had babies.

The thought was that since women *could* have children, they *should*; and since they *did*, they must *want* to. Hence the idea that the only psychologically healthy woman is the woman who willingly accepts her biologically instinctive nature – her God-given nature – and bears children. I give you a sweet passage from Krafft-Ebing's *Psychopathia Sexualis* concerning menopause:

> In the sedate matron, this condition is of minor psychological importance, though it is noticeable. The biological change affects her but little if her sexual career has been successful, and loving children gladden the maternal heart.[2]

As for middle-aged men, Krafft-Ebing warns:

> . . . impotence impairs health, mental freshness, activity, self-confidence and imagination . . . The sudden loss of the virile powers often produces melancholia, or is the cause of suicide when life without love is a mere blank. In cases where the reaction is less pronounced, the victim is morose, peevish, egotistical, jealous, narrow-minded, cowardly, devoid of energy, self-respect and honour. . . . This matter will be further elucidated under the heading of "Effemination."[3]

For all this, even Viagra can only do so much. And even if a lessening of sexual energy doesn't drive a man to commit suicide, he'll become effeminate, like a woman – a fate too awful to contemplate. For a woman, having children is her only source of genuine happiness and her only necessary sexual function.

In 1875, Dr. George Napheys of Philadelphia published a little book called *The Physical Life of Woman: Advice to the Maiden, Wife, and Mother*. Dr. Napheys was actually a man ahead of his time, for while recognizing how different the sexes were in their respective physiologies, he argued for their moral equality (within those God-given limits, of course). For example, Dr. Napheys explained that the reason why girls and women cannot throw a ball with the same accuracy as a man is only physical, because her shoulders are set farther back than his, giving her greater breadth of chest in front. This is why she is graceful in other things but not in throwing a ball. (Try this, ladies, and you will see how those mammaries block your follow-through.)

But "beyond all else," – and here Dr. Napheys waxes quite eloquent – woman "has the attributes of maternity, she is provided with organs to nourish and protect the child before and after birth."[4] Since she has these attributes, she had better use them, a point on which Dr. Napheys is so clear as to be downright threatening. It is a terrible thing for a woman *not* to have children, for then she flouts nature and God, and it is an unspeakable horror for her to commit "the crime of abortion." It is "better, far better," says the doctor, to "bear a child every year for twenty years than to resort to such a wicked and injurious step; better to die, if needs be, in the pangs of childbirth, than to live with such a weight of sin on the conscience."[5]

All of this may sound pretty bleak to twenty-first century ears, but then again, just how far have we come since 1875 in our understanding and expectations of gender roles and sex?

Jung was born in the year George Napheys' book was published. He began his work at the Burghölzli Hospital in Zurich in the year that Queen Victoria died (1901). As much a product of his time as anyone, Jung's pioneering work is all the more admirable, as he struggled to move beyond the bounds of nineteenth-century Victorian psychology, his mind ranging far afield and downward into the unmapped depths of the psyche. But part of him stayed "home," within the limits of the cultural perspectives and biases of his familiar European male world. Much of his cultural world is also ours, and while much has changed, much has not, or not changed enough. The work not yet done involves freeing Jung's archetypal theory and splendid vision of the psyche from genderizations. This is especially necessary in Jung's ideas about the animus, where most of his bias is visible.

There is no doubt that we owe a great debt to Jung for articulating and amplifying the idea that human sexuality cannot be separated from human spirituality; that sex is more than gratification of an instinctual drive and more than a blind, though passionate, urge to fullfil the biological imperative to reproduce. One of Jung's great contributions to psychology was just this recognition of the importance of the spiritual dimension of the human psyche, and the realization that no individual approaches the fullness of psychological life without incorporating that dimension.

In emphasizing the psychological importance of religious concerns, Jung reminds us that the physical is not only or merely the physical – that matter and the material world are just one dimension and never isolated from the life of the soul and the life of the spirit. What is important is that one *perceives* and *experiences* the spiritual dimension and significance to all happenings of life, that one is *open* to the numinous, through whatever activity or avenue it may come, including sex. As Christine Downing phrased it in her book, *Myths and Mysteries of Same-Sex Love*, Jung "reminds us to ask what age-old image of transformation or fulfillment is being reenacted here."[6]

But while Jung urged integration of the important factor of religion into psychological life, there is, in his work, an emphasis on the symbolic and the spiritual which subtly leads away from the actual and the material, perpetuating the age-old devaluation of the body and keeping us split off from it – as if one worships with the mind and soul, but not with the body; as if the making of prayer and the making of love could not be identical. Or, as if the *idea* of sex was of greater spiritual significance than the *act* of sex. As if sex belonged *only* to the body, and not to the spirit in its lofty aspirations. As if the *physical* dimension of making love was somehow less symbolic, less noble, less conducive to individuation than the *spiritual* dimension of making love. As if the union of psychic opposites is more truly unifying than the union of physical genitals. Or as if the rare mystery of the conjunction is more serious than the frequent humor of sexual engagement.

One of the reasons I am deliberately speaking here in terms of "sex" and "sexuality," instead of "eros," is because in Jungian psychology, the word and idea of "eros" has been made to carry too much of the spiritual and not enough of the physical. Jung's concept of eros as the "principle of relatedness" keeps it in the conceptual realm of principles, cut off from passion and body heat – keeps it desexualized, or asexual: the erotic subordinated to the mental or spiritual; the specifically sexual lost in the generalized context of relationship.

I do not mean that the sexual is always or only literal; but I do mean that sexuality must always include the physical reality of how things feel in and to the body, in the same way that what is truly erotic has a physical and affective component, and is not purely relational. In the film *Amadeus*, there is a very beautiful, passionate exchange in one of the last scenes – which was perhaps a sexual encounter of the third kind. Mozart is dying, he's very ill and delirious, and Salieri, the long-time court composer, comes to see him. Salieri has been jealous of Mozart for years, his own talent having been eclipsed by Mozart's genius. Now, standing at the foot of his archrival's deathbed, Salieri is asked by the dying man to write down the music for a Requiem, as Mozart hears it in his head and feverishly speaks it. So Salieri sits down and takes up pen and paper, and, in the writing, enters Mozart, begins to respond rhythmically to the movements of Mozart's mind – he becomes the physical agent of Mozart's passionate ejaculation of the music. It is a coupling, a moment of intense eroticism, sexually arousing. Here is a fascinating, and alien, image of two men making erotic love without touching through music that is not yet played.

The operative question here is *not* the usual Jungian one of *meaning*, but of sensate, physical *feeling*. The question that needs asking is not, "What does it *mean* to be gay or straight," not "What does it *mean* to be a man, or woman, or to be bisexual," or "What is the *meaning* of adultery, or intimacy, or anal intercourse," or "What is the meaning of clitoral as opposed to vaginal orgasm?" The question is: what do these images *feel* like in my body? If you're a man, what does sexually touching a man's penis feel like in your palm, or mouth? If you're a woman, what does a woman's breast feel like against your cheek or lips? What does your body feel when it does whatever it *usually* does in sexual encounters? What does it feel like in your body *not* to be sexually active?

It is not surprising that Jung placed human sexuality within the construct of "anima/animus," as a way of understanding physical sex through the soul of man (anima) and the spirit of woman (animus). One gets the distinct impression, reading Jung, and especially reading first and even second generation Jungian analysts, that if a man has a soul and a woman has spirit, what need is there for literal, actual sex? In terms of interpersonal relationships, his soul and her spirit make a marriage; in intrapsychic terms, his masculine ego and feminine soul make a marriage, or her feminine ego and masculine spirit make a marriage. (I might point out here that the *intra*psychic is probably the more economical way to go, since it requires only one literal person to make a marriage instead of two.)

We have to look at two major problems in Jung's work about sex: one is the pervasive genderism – his insistence on seeing just about everything in terms of a masculine/feminine dichotomy. And second, we have to separate female sexuality from the animus construct in which it is imprisoned.

The propensity to genderize is found in all areas of human culture (not only in psychology), but it starts in the psyche. Genderizing is a psychic fantasy. Historically, it has been the dominant psychic fantasy. And the propensity has continued explicitly in psychology, where much psychological theory has been based on assumptions about gender. Jung was not the only theorist to make gender assumptions, of course; but he is one of the earliest to articulate male/female paradigms and one of the most eloquent in describing the content and dynamics of gender differences, which he understood as psychic personifications and called "anima" and "animus."

However, Jung overlooked the fact that female sexuality is more complex than men's because it has been more severely repressed and denied, and because it has been made subservient to the functions of childbearing and relationship.

It is important to remember, too, that when we talk about male or female sexuality, we are talking about sex from a heterosexual perspective, which is as limiting and potentially inaccurate as talking about female sexuality from a male point of view. We are amazingly unconscious of heterosexism and how it skews our thinking about sexuality. This is why the newspapers have an article at least once a week on "what causes homosexuality" – as if we *already know* what "causes" *hetero*sexuality. Our unconsciousness also partly accounts for a long-standing confusion between sexuality and reproduction: we know quite a bit more about biological sexual reproduction than we do about psychological sexual pleasure. We really know very little about how the complexities of erotic arousal, intimacy, fear, shame, the need for beauty, and the politics of gender come together in nearly every coupling.

Jung's animus theory assumes a close association between a woman's inner male figure and her sexuality. He calls the anima and animus the "contrasexual" figures in the psyche, the psychical images of the opposite sex. For Jung, the animus is that psychical personification of all things masculine, formed from the collective heritage of woman's experience of men and from her own individual experiences with men, beginning with her father. The "real" man that most closely embodies her animus figure is likely to be the source of her sexual attraction; or, if the animus is "negative," she will be repelled by real men who constellate that negativity in her. In other words, an actual man that embodies the most alluring qualities of a woman's animus is expected to be romantically and sexually attractive to her.

But the "animus" really doesn't have much to do with a woman's sexuality or erotic interest. Animus is *not* associated with an image of the female body; neither is it an image of a woman's soul, which is female. The psychic figure of a woman's own female sexuality – whatever form that takes – is just as influential in her attraction to a sexual partner as the contrasexual male figure in her psyche. And I think this is so for heterosexual women as well as lesbians. Whether a woman enjoys the sexual energy of male bodies or female bodies, what attracts her is the person who highlights and intensifies her own female sexual self, and this may happen with a woman *or* a man. "Animus," as Jung formulated the concept, has nothing much to do with sexual passion and physical desire. In fact, *Jung's concept of "animus" forces us to look at female sexuality through the prism of male spirituality.*

We also have to consider that "contrasexuality" means not only the figure of opposite sex in the psyche; as Jung conceived it – and he coined the term – "contrasexuality" also means "heterosexuality." The powerful cultural bias in favor of *hetero*sexuality is deeply embedded in Jung's theory of anima/animus as the "*contra*sexual" archetypes. We cannot over-estimate the effect this heterosexist bias has on every one of us: in the way in which we think about sexuality, in the way in which we imagine our own sex fantasies, experience adolescence, perceive our bodies, and not least, all the ways in which we are inhibited from becoming conscious of any sort of sexual inclination which is not heterosexual.

Sexual attraction is something everyone experiences but no one can quite define. Sometimes it has to do with chemistry and physics, a physical sensation of tension seeking release, or an unspeakably wonderful, possibly shocking, sometimes sudden rearrangement of all your molecules. Or it erupts as the raw impulse to touch, stroke, grab, squeeze, press, caress – the soul in its most tactile form, urgently wanting, and wanting body. Sometimes sexual attraction comes from the stimulus of beauty, an aesthetic response of the genitals as well as the heart. Sometimes it has to do with alchemical secrets, dangerous and satisfying operations done with secretions, fluids, and flesh. Sometimes it has to do with the desire for "gnosis," the lust to know someone so intensely that it is impossible to tell where the body stops and the soul begins. And sometimes sexual arousal has to do with all sorts of "perversion:" bondage, whippings, slavery, compulsion, degradation. Each one of us has to find out what turns us on, and then we know what sexual attraction is. And all these things that have to do with sexual attraction have nothing to do with what gender you identify with, or what anatomical sex you are.

Our culture habitually and automatically puts sexual attraction and otherness together, and equates "sexual other" with "sexual opposite." Not only do we assume that the Other is the opposite, we also assume it "naturally" makes for sexual attraction, and therefore must be male in the case of a woman, and female in the case of a man. This was Jung's primary assumption. "Contrasexuality" means heterosexuality: not homosexuality, not bisexuality, no alien abductions to the third kind. Contrasexuality forces us to speak of sexuality in the singular, only one kind, rather than of "sexualities" plural, imagining a variety of sexual dimensions and encounters of many kinds, sometimes having only a coincidental connection to biological sex and social gender, or perhaps no connection at all.

We are so accustomed to thinking of "otherness" as a radical difference of kind – "other" as complete opposite – that we forget it might also be a difference of degree – otherness subtly differentiated along a continuum of similarity. It rarely occurs to us that alchemical conjunctions may happen between "sames" as well as between "opposites." We hardly ever imagine that individuation may take place through unions of affinities as well as through unions of opposites, that consciousness comes through recognition of likenesses as well as dissimilars.

The root assumption of Jung's anima/animus theory as contrasexual figures is that we are all, *by nature*, heterosexual beings by inclination as well as capability: that heterosexuality is the beginning and central point of reference for understanding all human sexuality. Of course, since Jung saw heterosexuality everywhere, his hypothesis of animus and anima as the makers of contrasexual projections are thus self-fullfilling definitions. And like Jung, we see heterosexuality (contrasexuality) everywhere, not so much because it is natural and universal, but because it is the only kind of sexuality for which our culture allows full visibility and approval. It is legally and socially easier to make a case for the sale of pornographic magazines showing mutilated women than to defend a lesbian's job as a school teacher or a gay army officer's distinguished service record. We have monosex, as we have monotheism.

The last thirty years, in particular, of the efforts of women to free themselves from introjected male ideas have gone a long way to righting the most blatant wrongs and inaccuracies in Jung's thinking about male-female stereotypes, and in psychology's genderism as well. But the idea of heterosexuality as normative for all behavior and *desire* is so deeply rooted in our collective psyche that it is truly a daunting task to dig down that far. All of us collectively and unconsciously still inhale the toxic fumes of homophobia – "fear of sames" – making institutional hetero-sexuality perhaps the last bastion of patriarchal moralism. Misogyny and homophobia go together: fear of women, fear of women who are imagined to be "unnaturally" like men, fear of men who are imagined to be "like women." At the famous Greek Orthodox monastery at Mount Athos, for example, a rule forbids entry to any woman, female animal, eunuch, or smooth person (male homosexual) – as if these are all the same thing. Here is an instance of the realization of Krafft-Ebing's dread warning about "effemination" of the man whose virility is diminished.

So pervasive is the fear of "effemination" that advertizing agencies play on it to sell products and causes, even good causes. A recent nation-wide public service advertisement encouraging people to be responsible pet owners by neutering their cats and dogs found it necessary to assure owners that "neutering" did not mean "demasculinizing." The copy reads: "Neutering your dog won't turn him into a sissy. No, your four-legged stud will be the same manly thing after being neutered as he was before. He'll still be as territorial. Still be a great watchdog. Still be, you know, a *guy*."

Jung considered homosexuality incongruent with an *adult* sexual adaptation. Along with the collective mind, he deems all non-heterosexual forms of sexuality as developmentally incomplete, psychologically deficient, and socially unadapted. And though he recognizes the symbolic value of homosexuality as inner homoeroticism, and the occasional psychological necessity for some people, particularly adolescents, to go through a homosexual period, Jung does not consider it either mature or "normal" to stay there.

But why must sex be "contra?" Talking about sex primarily in terms of contrasexuality keeps the shadow side unconscious: sex as "contra," "against," and "in opposition to," with the attendant associations and feelings of contrariness, hostility, violence, and anxiety.

Describing anima/animus as "contrasexual" not only locks us into literal gender thinking, it also forces us to make arbitrary and moralistic assignments as to where one's sexual interests *ought* to be placed: for the woman, always in the man; for the man, always in the woman. If an individual *refuses* the cultural assignment, or *fails* in carrying it out, we assume the presence of pathology: a negative mother complex in gay men, a negative animus in lesbians, various borderline pathologies in bisexual women or men. Or we assume a willful immorality, a stubborn refusal to live in accordance with one's God-given nature, for which the just punishment is either premature death from AIDS or eternal death in hell, or both. Given these strictures, the divine figure of Eros, whom the Greeks called the first-born and fairest of the Gods, is quarantined in the heterosexual complex of the psyche, limited to sexual encounters of the first and second kinds only. And this limitation on Eros has been nearly fatal to romance, to sexual aesthetics, and certainly to a deeper understanding of human sexuality.

Heterosexuality is the locus of one of our culture's root neuroses, the place where we are adamantly one-sided, that is, unconscious. Since usually it is only life's "aberrations" that catch our attention, whatever is defined as "normal" tends to be taken for granted: *whatever is considered "normal" is that of which we are unconscious.* (I once heard "normal" correctly defined as "a vegetative state in which nothing happens.")

Heterosexism and its correlate, homophobia, are the great defenses against the marvelous freedom and allure of the psychic figure Freud called the "polymorphously perverse child," which Jungians have transformed into the asexual divine child. In keeping with our culture's Christian wish to see the child as divine on one hand, and our frightening ambivalence about real children on the other, the psychic figure of the "child" has been stripped of all sexual possibilities (except when literalized by adult perpetrators of sexual crimes). Polymorphous sexual possibilities are projected on to bisexuals, who then appear to be like children who can't make up their minds, on to transgender people who are not to be taken seriously because they appear to act like children who like to cross-dress, and on to homosexuals, in whom sex is perceived as childish and perverse. If we accept the premise that heterosexuality is the primary orientation of all human beings, the norm of practice, the natural desire, and the goal of relational maturity, we must conclude that *everyone* individuates in the same direction, doing, feeling, and wanting the same sort of sexual and relational life as everyone else. In a stroke, the process of individuation becomes the process of collectivization.

Our failure, or refusal, to consider dimensions of sexual experience other than heterosexuality is a form of severe repression from which we *all* suffer. Such failure relegates a vast territory of the sexual imagination to a corner of the psyche labeled immature, stuck, regressive, sick or at least disturbed, and depending on one's religious orientation, immoral. For women especially, whose sexuality has been historically so consistently denied, repressed, degraded, punished or restricted, the discovery of and loyalty to one's deepest erotic desires, the willingness to follow one's uncharted path into sexual realms disallowed for at least two thousand years, is no small act of courage.

It has been thought by many psychologists and also some Jungians, that gays, lesbians, and bisexuals are incapable of full individuation because their sexual orientation is really *dis*oriented, eros turned away from its "true" and "natural" goal. But heterosexual people have been at a real disadvantage in that they are not *required* to wrestle with questions of their own sexual identity. To the extent that a heterosexual identity is taken for granted, to that extent it remains unconscious. Heterosexuals who do not reflect upon the nature of their own sexual inclination remain unconscious of all the collective assumptions about heterosexuality, and are thus forced to accept them by default: that heterosexuality is really all there is, the whole thing and not just a part; that it means adulthood and maturity; that it is wondrously satisfying and prevents loneliness; that it cures sexual rejection and inadequacy complexes; that it is the golden archway to romantic love; that such unions are a foretaste of immortality because they are not merely a phase and so will last forever; that human psychosexuality and human reproduction go together as an obvious law of nature; and, most insidiously, that since heterosexuality is the universal norm, then anyone who is *not* heterosexual has consciously *chosen* to flout the law of nature.

Consider this last assumption: heterosexuality is not an individual conscious decision, a sexual "lifestyle" selected from among many possibilities. On the contrary: all our cultural institutions work to compel it, our laws to preserve it, our psychologies to normalize it, our arts to glorify it, our religions to sanction it. Why so much effort to compel heterosexuality if it is already the natural orientation?

We have yet to go very far below the surface of human sexuality, which is surely one of the most complicated, if not the *most* complex, aspects of our being. While I believe we have a gift of inestimable value from Jung in his archetypal theory, which teaches us *how* to perceive the depth and mythic resonance and human commonality of psychological experience, we must go beyond, or below, even his extraordinary range of vision.

It is time for imagining sexual encounters of the third kind, making welcome guests of sexual fantasies and figures who appear in the psyche as "alien," and allowing ourselves to be abducted by them, taken up or down into realms barely hinted at in our customary notions of sex. When Hamlet says, "There are more things in heaven and earth, Horatio, than are dreamt of in your philosophy," he has made the first move necessary for any individuation process: he has noticed that *there is more*.

We may have to begin imagining sexual encounters of the third kind by finding new ways of imagining gender and the expectations we have of gender images. Imagine that, instead of the Great Mother as the ultimate image of femaleness, we had the Great Woman – not the mother, not the daughter, not the whore, not the virgin, not the girl, not the wife, not the mistress, or any other designation by which she is defined in relation to men. Just the Great Woman. In fact, just Woman, to indicate a central point of reference as we now use "man," a category under which woman is subsumed. Imagine that women enjoyed sex just because it was fun, for its own sake, purely for the sake of the body's pleasure, and less because it served or expressed relationship.

Psychology has always looked at sexual pleasure in terms of gratifica-tion, tension, and release, and hardly ever in terms of sensual, physical, erotic pleasure, in spite of Freud's elevation of pleasure to the status of a principle. Imagine *women* writing psychologically about sex not in terms of gratification, tension, potency, but in terms of beauty, pleasure and desire, sensuality, climax – and that such writing is neither stereotypically romance novel, nor traditional pornography, nor political polemic. After all, it is the woman who has a clitoris, which has as its sole and noble purpose the experience of pleasure. Imagine, along with Robert Bly's cult of the phallus, we had a cult of the clitoris. Imagine women writing their own clitoral, not literal, psychology.

Imagine we all agreed that sex should be private because it has to do with a female sense of interiority, not because it has to do with guilt or shame. Imagine what it would be like if we valued masturbation as a way of practicing differentiation and refinement of individual sexual pleasure, instead of regarding it as narcissistic, or lamenting its necessity in the absence of an actual relationship. Imagine how psychologically free we could be if all the simple expressions of desire and love and sexual affection were *everywhere visible*: two men kissing on a park bench; two women holding hands in a quiet restaurant; teenage boys dancing together at a rock concert; Thelma and Louise, larger than life on the movie screen, making raucous love on the car's back seat instead of going over the cliff's edge in the front seat.

Imagine what might happen if we began to think of sexual promiscuity as merely boring. Imagine sensual interest in another person that is not harassment; imagine delight in the sexual awakening of children that is not incestuous, not guilt-ridden, not exploitive. Imagine sex having nothing to do with power; imagine rape having nothing to do with sex. Think of all the sexual possibilities and encounters we *don't* see, and you begin to get a sense of how impoverished our sexual imagination is, and how hard it is for us to venture out from the old, the usual, the customary, the habitual, the "normal." Don't forget: most people who claim to have seen UFOs, not to mention the aliens in them, are usually dismissed as kooks, or at least a little queer.

In the last century we have had two revolutions initiated by women: the first came in the 1920s when women got the vote in America, left the Victorian invention called "the home," went to work, and threw off the restraints of corset and convention. Then, after the catastrophic regression of the 1950s, the second revolution came in the late 1960s-early '70s. The first revolution had to do primarily with political and economic freedom (and that revolution is far from over); the second revolution had to do with intellectual and sexual freedom (and *that* revolution is far from over).

I think the next revolution – starting, I hope, no later than next week – must be a radical exploration of the sexual imagination, encounters with "alien" images that live within us, a free and honest search for images of human sexuality that will teach us in the deepest ways, perhaps not so much about actual sex, but about what it means to love, to take delight in whatever is different – from all the rich flavors of ice cream to all the rich colors of human skin. In short, to find out more of what it means to be truly human.

Notes

1. Richard von Krafft-Ebing, *Psychopathia Sexualis*, New York: Stein and Day, 1965, p. 3.
2. Ibid., p. 8.
3. Ibid.
4. George Napheys, *The Physical Life of Woman: Advice to the Maiden, Wife, and Mother*, Philadelphia, 1875, p. 20.
5. Ibid., p. 23.
6. Christine Downing, *Myths and Mysteries of Same-Sex Love*, New York: Continuum, 1989, p.127.

Chapter 10

Blue notes

Some reflections on melancholy

I will say nothing against the course of my existence. But at bottom it has been nothing but pain and burden, and I can affirm that during the whole of my 75 years, I have not had four weeks of genuine well-being. It is but the perpetual rolling of a rock that must be raised up again forever.

(Goethe, *Conversations with Goethe* in
The Varieties of Religious Experience)

For healthy people, life is only an unconscious and unavowed flight from the consciousness that one day one must die. Illness is always a warning and a trial of strength. And so illness, pain, suffering are the most important sources of religious feeling.

(Kafka, *I Am a Memory Come Alive*)

My name is Lyn and I'm a melancholic. And since I associate the melancholic temperament with intellectual passion, sensual eroticism, and creative genius, I am not interested in being cured. In fact, I am advertising melancholy as a partial cure for cultural mania, a collective condition which our culture considers normal. I am putting forth melancholy as a natural, homeopathic remedy for the murderous superficiality and pathological speed that characterizes our society, and that prevents psychological maturation.

As far as contemporary mainstream psychology and the culture in general is concerned, clearly the romance has gone out of melancholy. We don't have unrequited love, we have co-dependency. We don't have deep longings, we have addictions. We don't recognize real failure in our lives, we merely regret poor choices. Most of our great passions have become disorders.

So, for the sake of this most ancient of human afflictions, I want to consider melancholy in two ways: first, as an antidote to cultural mania;

Melancolia I, engraving by Albrecht Dürer, 1517. Courtesy of the Herbert F. Johnson Museum of Art. Bequest of William P. Chapman Jr., Class of 1895 (57.122)

and second, as a distinct mood, personified and animating, that can be a matrix of creative work: that is, the Muse personified and imagined as a majestic womanly figure known in the Renaissance as Dame Melancholy.

Jung thought that melancholy was the pathology of introversion, a too-extreme withdrawal of energy from the world. And while melancholics are known to be solitary in their individual sorrow, we find a historical community of like-minded souls in the Western world (which is my intellectual community), stretching back at least to Aristotle.

Although the content and context of our melancholic mournings are different from age to age and person to person, there is much that is amazingly similar, such as the nature of this sorrow itself, the quality of grief, the preoccupation with philosophic questions of desperate import (suicide, despair, the meaning of life), and peculiar traits of character. These traits historically include but are not limited to: a great capacity for work, intellectual brilliance, sullen fits, temper tantrums, a talent for leadership, and a tendency to constipation.

In ancient Greece, melancholy was recognized as one of the four natural temperaments – sanguine, phlegmatic, bilious, and melancholic – based on the four humors of the body: blood, phlegm, yellow bile, and black bile. The preponderance of one of these humors over the others made for a characteristic temperament: the preponderance of phlegm, for example, produced a phlegmatic temperament. The preponderance of blood made one sanguine.

Of the four temperaments, the melancholic was the one thought to be "touched with genius" by the gods, consumed with intellectual passion, and most prone to madness. In the European Christianity of the Middle Ages melancholy was regarded as a serious sin, called "acedia," perhaps best translated as "spiritual despair," and a particular affliction of monks and nuns. In the later Middle Ages, "acedia" lost its deeper meaning and became a behavioral vice called "sloth." In the Renaissance, which looked back to the classical Greek conception of melancholy as the temperament of genius, this complex condition was personified in the figure of Dame Melancholy, a woman of contained power, a divine Muse.

As a person of melancholic temperament myself, I feel more in harmony sometimes with a medieval nun than with most contemporary get-happy, feel-good mental health professionals. And I am not even Catholic. The fact that my temperament finds no psychological or intellectual home in my own time is, I think, more a comment on the state of my profession than on the state of my mind. For once psychology abandons psyche to relentless good feeling, and makes emotional comfort the goal and highest value of therapy, it also abandons one of the Muses, Dame Melancholy, and thus psychology loses its genius for attending the human soul in its extremity. A psychology that can only see "melancholia" as a clinical depressive disorder is itself showing symptoms of manic optimism.

In our day, Dame Melancholy has become less than a shadow of her former majestic self. She has been reduced to "depression," depersonified into a "major depressive disorder," as it is called in the *Diagnostic and Statistical Manual*, the primary manual used by psychiatrists and psychologists. And even then, she is included as a "qualifier," an add-on feature making things even worse than just "depressed." The qualities that distinguish melancholy – its slowness, its wry sense of irony, its bittersweetness and nostalgia, its sad romanticism, its love of history, its existential pessimism – all have been subsumed and undifferentiated in the diagnostic category of "depression." And because these qualities conflict with the basic Western, and especially American, ideals of health and progress, the dark visage of Dame Melancholy in the modern psyche is conceived as a symptom of sickness instead of perceived as the womanly face of wisdom and slow care.

We live in a world where speed is of the essence; in our hurry to get to the better future, we forget or haven't noticed that the quick fix is no antidote for the slow wound. In a speed-oriented culture like ours, ruled by the child archetype that keeps us convinced we must have instant gratification, haste lays waste to the normal periodicities and seasons of life, those slow-turning cycles necessary for maturation, security, solidity, and *lasting* change. In a world where everything must happen instantly – instant copies, instant replay, instant e-mail, instant election returns – of course no one can keep up. It is like Alice in Wonderland, who has been running herself to exhaustion with the Red Queen and finally notices they have gotten nowhere at all. The Red Queen tells Alice something important about this upside down world: "Now, here, you see, it takes all the running you can do, to keep in the same place. If you want to get somewhere else, you must run at least twice as fast as that!" So we run twice as fast keeping in touch, accessible anywhere, anytime, through the fax, the car phone, the pager – and then wonder why we feel so out of touch and no longer know how to talk deeply about important things that matter to us. We process billions of words at blinding speed, but what are we saying? No wonder that cocaine, giving an instant high, is so popular, and that "speed" is still the national drug of choice.

With the arrival of Prozac, and the culture of psychological mediocrity in which it proliferates, the hope and vision of a well-rounded life that includes the downside as well as the upbeat fades and recedes. This form of drug dependency points to a situation in which our moods, chemically made lighter, are also made psychologically meaningless, mood without image or import. No wonder more and more of us are getting more and more depressed.

But, as with most poorly understood or prejudged psychological afflictions, there are gifts in melancholy, three of which are *thinking*, *memory*, and *nostalgia*. These are useful and even necessary for creative work.

Since ancient times melancholy has been recognized as a scourge that yet brings gifts to those souls who are called to become poets, artists, philosophers, mystics, psychologists, architects, and statesmen/women. While these fields of study (art, literature, philosophy, religion, politics) are not identical with each other, they all share an affinity of spirit: melancholy is an affliction of the liberal arts. In this tradition, beginning in ancient Greece and still extant in the heart of every romantic, it is expected that melancholy accompanies great achievements in these fields, and in some sense is a necessary precondition for them. The list is long of those so accursedly gifted: Beethoven, Churchill, Lincoln, Michelangelo, Billie Holiday, Virginia Woolf, the prophet Jeremiah, Martin Luther, Simone Weil, William James, Alice James (William's sister), Toulouse-Lautrec, Anne Sexton, probably Freud, the Virgin Mary, and on and on. Most of what we call culture is made by melancholics.

In the Renaissance, it was understood that too much *thinking* made one melancholy. It was not just that much learning, study, and scholarship was taxing on the brain, it was also that these heady pursuits *changed* you – changed your attitude toward life, and led to thoughts that heavily burdened the soul. In the Book of Ecclesiastes (1:18) the preacher says, "For in much wisdom is much vexation, and he who increases knowledge increases sorrow," and he was right. The deeper one thinks about important matters, the more melancholic one is likely to become. The poet John Keats urged the nightingale to take its sweet song far away from that place in the soul "where but to think is to be full of sorrow and leaden-eyed despairs." Thinking and optimism do not naturally go together. And of course there is the trenchant remark of Archy the Cockroach, the creation and companion of newspaper columnist Don Marquis, who wrote in the 1920s. (Archy was actually a philosopher who, through an accident of reincarnation, came back in the form a cockroach, and thus is known as the Vermin Voltaire.) Archy gave us this astute definition of the optimist who is not inclined to reflective thought: "An optimist is a guy that ain't never had very much experience."

In Renaissance thinking it was expected that education, learning, study, should change you, and change you into a melancholic. And thus melancholy was understood as an attribute of *maturity*, both intellectual and psychological, because it represented the fruition of long years of disciplined mental effort, resulting in a changed world-view. What may have begun as an optimistic view of life in youth becomes more pessimistic the more one thinks about it. The early twentieth-century American psychologist William James thought of this "change of mind" as much like a religious conversion, and described the melancholic as a "twice-born" soul.

But it is hard to *think* these days; everything mitigates against it. Most obviously, there is an intellectual vacuum at nearly all levels of political leadership and in the glibness of hundreds of radio and television talk-shows, where hardly an intricate, creative thought is heard. *Mental* exercise cannot compete with video aerobics and fitness work-outs. In psychotherapy, the preferred therapeutic question is, "How do you *feel* about it?" rather than, "What do you *think*?" Even cognitive therapy, by putting thinking in the service of a predetermined goal, steers the melancholic soul *away* from its deep longing to wallow in reflective, meandering thought. The two favored American goals of therapy, particularly for depressed people, is either to "get your mind off it," whatever "it" is; or, to find a solution to a problem that is preconceived as a problem – and do it as fast as possible. This goal-oriented approach keeps us on the go and on the surface, and produces lots of solutions but very little understanding. The old popular advice to get your mind off depressing things is a form of anti-intellectualism, a distrust of deep or serious mental activity, as well as a kind of magical thinking: don't think about it and it won't happen; or conversely, thinking makes it so, so stop thinking.

But such distrust belies a deep belief in the power of thought to change us, change our attitudes – as if, if we really thought deeply about ourselves, thought reflectively more than logically, we would find out awful truths, would feel terrible, or worse than terrible: uncomfortable. We would be forced to change in the very core of our being. Unlike cognitive therapy, which helps us think differently about things, I want us to think about different things. I am referring to the kind of deep, thoughtful reflection that moves us out of the horizontal ego-world of problems and into the vertical world of soul concerns. I am suggesting that while reflective thoughtfulness may induce melancholy, it may also relieve "depression."

Such reflective thinking may also be extremely fruitful and helpful, by providing a quiet state in which, as the great writer Toni Morrison puts it, one can "hear things." In reponse to an interviewer's question: "When did you know you were a writer," Morrison replied:

> After I had written *Sula*. I've said I wrote *The Bluest Eye* after a period of depression, but the words "lonely, depressed, melancholy"

don't really mean the obvious. They simply represent a different state. It's an unbusy state, when I am more aware of myself than of others. The best words for making that state clear to other people are those words. It's not necessarily an unhappy feeling; it's just a different one. I think now I know better what that state is. Sometimes when I'm in mourning, for example, after my father died, there's a period when I'm not fighting day-to-day battles, a period when I can't fight or don't fight, and I am very passive, like a vessel. When I'm in this state, I can hear things. As long as I'm busy doing what I should be doing, what I'm supposed to be doing, what I must do, I don't hear anything; there isn't anything there. This sensibility occurred when I was lonely or depressed or melancholy or idle or emotionally exhausted. I would think I was at my nadir, but it was then that I was in a position to hear something. Ideas can't come to me while I'm preoccupied. This is what I meant when I said I was in a state that was not busy, not productive or engaged. It happened after my father died, thus the association with depression. It happened after my divorce. It has happened other times, but not so much because I was unhappy or happy. It was that I was unengaged, and in that situation of disengagement with the day-to-day rush, something positive happened. I've never had sense enough to deliberately put myself in a situation like that before. At that time I had to be put into it. Now I know how to bring it about without going through the actual event.[1]

The second aspect of melancholy is *memory*. According to the Greek medical theory of the four humors, melancholy (which means, literally, "black bile") was thought to produce the best memory, because black bile is a "cold and dry" humor. So the condition of melancholy is excellent for storage, working like a refrigerator, and the melancholic was thought to receive memory impressions or images more firmly, and retain them longer, than other temperaments. This does not mean that the *content* of memory was experienced as "good" and "pleasurable," but that the *faculty* of memory, the ability to remember, worked better in melancholics than in other humoral dispositions.

Memory, named Mnemosyne by the ancient Greeks who knew her as a goddess, is the mother of the Muses, those mythic persons that generate art, music, history, and poetry. And so Memory is also the mother of the Muse, Dame Melancholy, and the matrix from which all creative endeavors are born.

In modern times, memory too has become another example of Jung's saying that the "gods have become diseases." Like melancholy, Memory has become a disease: no longer a goddess and preserver of the images that solidify and make secure our histories, but a mere function, disturbing our peace, too intrusive, frustratingly elusive. Once-divine Memory has become a patient of modern American psychotherapy, abused or deceiving, needing to be recovered and released from repression. Mnemosyne, who was once greatly honored through her nine daughters, the Muses, now is hauled daily into courtrooms as well as consulting rooms, a defendant in the false-memory syndrome debate, accused of being unreliable, distorted, manipulative, contrived, giving "false" testimony.

Our modern psychological mistake, of course, has been to literalize memory, reducing her from person to function, associated with events, data, factual truth. But Memory is not much interested in mere record keeping, faultless accounts and accurate testimony. She is concerned with imaginal life, the life and preservation of images – even if those recollections have a slowing effect on us and pull us down into blue moods, gray lethargies, dark moments of near despair. In the course of psychic life, literal events by themselves count for relatively little – look at the paucity of literal events in the life of Emily Dickinson, or Marcel Proust who spent years in bed engaging in a remembrance of things past.

As a people, we Americans have a pronounced antipathy to history. History, after all, moves us back in time and down to a deeper perception of patterns at work – two directions Americans have always associated with wasteful regression. History also is a constant reminder of the fact of death, and that all things end. Americans by tradition and collective temperament have always been more interested in beginnings rather than endings; what has already come and gone does not interest a people whose face is always to the future. So naturally our national shadow grows darker and more depressive as it falls into ever-lengthening history, that graveyard of mostly untended markers in which are buried some of the deepest secrets of how we came to be the way we are. It is in this shadow that many melancholics live, largely unconsciously preserving the sense of history for the culture, struggling, and often unable, to make meaning of it.

Historically, the melancholic person was thought to have an excellent faculty of memory; but it was also ungovernable. It was well known that melancholics were uncontrolled in everything, greedy, driven by lust. (Plato, for example, puts melancholics, lovers and drunkards in the same category.) They have no command over their memory. They cannot remember what they want to when they want to; their memories bring things back intrusively, "unseasonably." Also, they tend to stutter or mix their words, since speech is slower than thought. Thus memory, as an uncontrollable, ungovernable faculty, capable of holding practically everything but yielding nothing in its wanted season, was both a great gift of melancholia and also part of its grievous affliction. Such a melancholic memory is like having an overstocked warehouse with no way of taking inventory.

This capricious quality of memory, then, worked in two ways: it made the melancholic person excessively irritable; and, it became characteristic of *genius*. The capacity to reproduce images of compelling force and with vivid emotional immediacy – as in a powerful painting or compelling novel – has no doubt contributed to the traditional equation of art and madness, the artist as tormented melancholic. This "agitated and crowded memory," as it was called, once awakened, could not be stopped, and took on the character of an obsession. The vehemence of the melancholic's imagination led to the association of "melancholia" with "passion." (In Arabic, for example, the words "black" and "melancholic" are both synonymous with "passion.")

In the early Middle Ages the alchemist and priest Albertus Magnus differentiated two types of melancholy. The first is the "cold and dry" type just described; the second kind, said Albertus, is "*hot* and dry." This is not "ordinary" melancholy, but intellectual, inspired melancholy. "Inspired melancholy" makes you mentally hot, heats the brain, and brings the mind to fever pitch. It is not an *emotional* heat, which only creates confusion in thinking, it is an intellectual fervor, a passion of the mind in ferment. And this is a good place to remember that the word "passion" comes from the Latin root meaning "to suffer." The idea that will not let you go, the poem that must be written, the theme running relentlessly through a musician's head, the political activist's world-changing plan, the psychologist's radical new theory – all these may be the compelling, gripping, igniting intellectual force that fuels itself on the black bile of melancholy.

Imagine memory, with all its images implanted, as the body or substance or content of one's melancholy. Or imagine memory as the container for these contents, as a cool dark vault housing a museum of precious memories, unfulfilled dreams as well as triumphs and small satisfactions; and there is a large room where one can visit the exhibits called, "What Might Have Been."

Imagine memory as a prison from which there is no escape and the term is life, a place where your life is lived again and again and there is no apparent progress. This is the prison of memories we can't forget though we desperately want to, memories that originate in our deepest wounds, which often are the genesis of both the deepest pathology and genuine creativity. These memories come back time and again, feeling almost like divine retribution for unknown or long-forgotten sins and crimes, even though we may have been truly innocent.

Memory is a place of equal delight and torment, and thus gives melancholy its characteristic bittersweet flavor. John Keats, the poet full of passion and dead at twenty-six, wrote these lines in his "Ode on Melancholy":

> . . . But when the melancholy fit shall fall
>   Sudden from heaven like a weeping cloud,
> That fosters the droop-headed flowers all,
>   And hides the green hill in an April shroud;
> Then glut thy sorrow on a morning rose,
>   Or on the rainbow of the salt sand-wave,
>   Or on the wealth of globed peonies; . . .
> She dwells with Beauty – Beauty that must die;
>   And Joy, whose hand is ever at his lips
> Bidding adieu; and aching Pleasure nigh,
>   Turning to poison while the bee-mouth sips:
> Ay, in the very temple of delight
>   Veil'd Melancholy has her sovran shrine,
>   Though seen of none save him whose strenuous tongue
>   Can burst Joy's grape against his palate fine;
> His soul shall taste the sadness of her might,
>   And be among her cloudy trophies hung.

The third aspect of melancholy is *nostalgia*, to which I am connecting the idea of "religious melancholy."

Dame Melancholy resides in the mature person who has something to be melancholic about: losses, many memories, faded dreams and glories, nostalgic history. She is not much concerned with youthful follies that pass in an instant or that can be smoothed over by an equally fleeting moment of pleasure. She is a heavy, solid, majestic woman; she wears a gown of thick, enduring fabric – an "April shroud" – not the cotton summer frock of a wispy Persephone amongst the flowers.

Her gaze, in Dürer's engraving (see p. 121), is directed at nothing in particular. Unlike youth, which looks at the immediate present, Melancholy looks back, or ahead, and always inward – but almost never at anything in particular. She is not goal-oriented, we would say in behavioral terms. Melancholy is a mood which colors all experience and events, but focuses on no one of them specifically. All things entering my blue melancholic mood become melancholic too, take on a blue or violet or gray cast. The song I hear on the radio, a friend's voice on the telephone, a sudden, fleeting memory from childhood, a distinctive smell I can't quite place, last night's dream feeling, thoughts for a new work project – all contribute to the mood by becoming part of it. Melancholy is a kind of shroud, a veil, or a pall; it is a reminder of the heaviness of mortality, and in some darkly profound way, it prepares one for death.

Perhaps this is why melancholy feels so close to nostalgia, a longing for something relatively unknown, or for a time long past or a time that never was, nor will be – yet the loss of it is so great that its absence lies like a stone in the heart.

What is longed for is hidden in the root meaning of the Greek word "nostalgia:" *nostos*, meaning "a return home," and *algia*, meaning "painful." Nostalgia means, literally, a painful return home; whatever home we long to return to is a source of pain precisely because we cannot return to it. "Home" may be that actual childhood home of family, or the Eden of innocence, or heaven, or that time and place where one first discovered love. If the effort to return is expended in work – serious, meaningful work – the pain may be endured even if the return cannot be accomplished. The Greeks had a saying that the Muses, daughters of Memory, can change the weave of Fate, suggesting that through creative work we find redemptive meaning, and can change the design, if not the fabric, of our lives. The term "melancholy" includes but does not adequately describe this quietly passionate nostalgic longing. This longing does not have a single name; it cannot truly be spoken. Historians call it "the Golden Age." Mystics call it the lost vision of God. Poets call it unrequited love. Psychoanalysis calls it the prenatal womb. Jungians call it the Great Mother, the timeless mythic, archetypal image of beginning and end. It is perhaps all of these, or none; what characterizes the longing is that the longed-for thing or place belongs in another dimension – not in *time* at all (past, future) but in timelessness.

Melancholic nostalgia is an eternal longing for that which is eternal. Melancholics mourn both mortality *and* the entrapment in time. We find in melancholy a mood that warps us into timelessness, and a reverie like a nostalgia for death. Melancholics are by nature and temperament especially vulnerable to painful nostalgia. It is often very difficult, if not impossible, to find meaning in this pain; so it is no surprise when a melancholic state of mind brings up thoughts of suicide – not so much as a result of "depression" over failure to be perfect or some other egocentric concern, but because *meaning* has failed: the ability to find meaning in life has failed. At bottom, there may be a close, even fatal link between melancholic nostalgia and the medieval affliction of "acedia," that terrible condition of spiritual despair so complete that one no longer cares about the fact that one no longer cares.

Having made this connection between nostalgia and spiritual despair, it is a small step to consider *melancholy as a religious attitude toward life*, an attitude of pessimism though not morbidity, an attitude that is rooted in a harshly realistic view of life without being necessarily defeatist.

In *The Varieties of Religious Experience*, William James described two very different temperaments. There is the "healthy-minded" temperament, and the "sick soul." James observed that the healthy-minded temperament "has a constitutional *in*capacity for prolonged suffering."[2] This is the temperament we call the eternal optimist, the sanguine personality who prefers and is always able to look on the bright and sunny side of life. By contrast the "sick soul" is found in those who, James wrote, "cannot so swiftly throw off the burden of the consciousness of evil, but are congenitally fated to suffer from its presence."[3] This is the melancholic temperament.

Neither of these temperamental attitudes are monolithic structures of personality; there are, says James, "shallower and profounder" levels of happiness in healthy-minded types, and there are varying degrees of "morbidity" in melancholics.

James himself was a melancholic, and in his study of the two contrary temperaments, he found the greater value, profundity, and complexity in the melancholic or pessimistic view. For him, as for all religious melancholics, the real question becomes not how to stop worrying or how to stop being pessimistic, but, *how can one realistically be anything else*?

> . . . How *can* things so insecure as the successful experiences of this world afford a stable anchorage? A chain is no stronger than its weakest link, and life is after all a chain. In the healthiest and most prosperous existence, how many links of illness, danger, and disaster are always interposed? Unsuspectedly from the bottom of every fountain of pleasure . . . something bitter rises up: a touch of nausea, a falling dead of the delight, a whiff of melancholy, things that sound a knell, for fugitive as they may be, they bring a feeling of coming from a deeper region and often have an appalling convincingness. The buzz of life ceases at their touch as a piano-string stops sounding when the damper falls on it.[4]

James, who turned fifty-nine as the nineteenth century became the twentieth, lived in a world where there were more than enough miseries and hardships to make one melancholic well before World War I, World War II, the Death Camps, the Bomb, globally threatening biological weapons. If optimism was indefensible then, it should have disappeared from the list of options by this time.

James distinguishes between "pathological melancholy" and "religious melancholy." *Pathological melancholy* is what we today call "agitated depression," with symptoms of insomnia, loss of appetite, impoverished thought and imagination, lack of concentration, feelings of guilt, and sorrow. *Religious melancholy* is not a set of symptoms but a philosophy, a world-view that arises out of an individual's natural temperament and experience of the world and herself in it. The religious task is then to affirm the authenticity of one's subjective experience. The way out of "pathological melancholy" is into religious melancholy, a "conversion" from "once-born" to the "twice-born" experience of oneself as a "sick soul," and this movement is what James calls a "process of redemption."

The entire value system on which the individual's life has been built changes in this "process of redemption." The loss of those values – many of them given through culture, society, religion, family – begins the descent, in fact, makes the descent both possible and necessary. All the impossible tortured questions of meaning explode into consciousness: "Why?", "Why me?", "What is this *for*?", "What does this *mean*?", "What next?" Tolstoy suffered this complete breakdown and though he did not *wish* to commit suicide, found that "the force which drew me away from life was fuller, more powerful, more general than any mere desire. It was a force like my old aspiration to live, only it impelled me in the opposite direction. It was an aspiration of my whole being to get out of life."[5]

When one suffers such a loss of meaning, of values, when one has been so impelled to death and aspires to get out of life, one cannot expect that a return to "health" will be merely a restoration of the way things were before. Such expectation sees "health" as "what you were used to," "the familiar." And significantly it is often in the *status quo* that the origin of the "sickness" is found. Using the religious vocabulary of evil and redemption, James observes:

> When disillusionment has gone as far as this, there is seldom a *restitutio ad integrum*. One has tasted of the fruit of the tree, and the happiness of Eden never comes again. The happiness that comes, when any does come, – and often enough it fails to return in an acute form, though its form is sometimes very acute, – is not the simple ignorance of ill, but something vastly more complex, including natural evil as one of its elements, but finding natural evil no such

stumbling-block and terror because it now sees it swallowed up in supernatural good. The process is one of redemption, not of mere reversion to natural health, and the sufferer, when saved, is saved by what seems to him a second birth, a deeper kind of conscious being than he could enjoy before.[6]

Modern psychology's preoccupation with symptoms of depression, its attitude of expediency, and its reliance on drugs in "treating" depression show an appalling superficiality in the face of real human suffering. The refusal of psychiatry certainly, and psychology generally, to regard depression as authentic melancholy, as one of James's varieties of religious experience – apart from whatever else it might be – is demeaning to the sufferer and perpetuates a violence against the soul that is already in torment.

How irrelevantly remote seem all our usual refined optimisms and intellectual and moral consolations in presence of a need of help like this! Here is the real core of a religious problem: Help! Help! No prophet can claim to bring a final message unless he says things that will have a sound of reality in the ears of victims such as these. But the deliverance must come in as strong a form as the complaint, if it is to take effect; and that seems a reason why the coarser religions, revivalistic, orgiastic, with blood and miracles and supernatural operations, may possibly never be displaced.[7]

Scientism is the religion of our time, with psychology one of its sects. And with its vapid, cultic jargon and love of diagnostic litanies, its apotropaic incense of a thousand drugs, proves James right: we would do far better with more coarseness, more "blood," more intensity, more passion, more depth. These are the antidotes to the deadening civilized structures and conventions which pass for both organized religion and professional psychology. We would probably do well to have a psychology of aspiration, of fervor for the soul which is its proper subject, of poetry, of serious and loving attention – a real therapy of the psyche. Like the less coarse, more "civilized" religions, psychology has been stripped of its Venusian sensuality, its blood-pulse and life-force, trivializing the soul's great sufferings. It understands the soul's need for redemption and great sacrificial dramas only in terms of wafer-thin concepts, approved for application by clerks in insurance companies who stare at computor monitors, following the cursor as if it were the finger of God pointing the way to salvation.

For the sake of melancholics who look to it for help, psychology should turn to the ancient Lord of Souls, Dionysus, who stands for everything the oppressive, depressive god Saturn fears: orgiastic driving of blood, the relentless pulse of life and sexual heat, a bisexual god who knows in his own divine being the madness and necessity of descent, the torment of abandonment and dismemberment, and the profoundly melancholic sorrow of realizing that he is, as we are, always Outcast.

Religious melancholy is, at its core, a stark, raw condition of inconsolable grief. Life is lived as if one were an exposed nerve; life is pain. One may indeed feel profound pleasure, but still be unable to turn away from pain. The heart works, but is forever broken. For the melancholic, there is endurance of suffering and its grief; and often much meaning to be found therein. There is occasional hope, but not much expectation; or there is madness, or death. But no cure.

The religious melancholic need not magnify pain and suffering; the fateful calling is to witness and endure, one's own pain, often others'. There is a Jewish tradition that tries to understand how a world so full of pain and anguish is able to continue. It is the Legend of the Just Men, but they are also women, and at any given time there are thirty-six of them in the world. The world rests upon them, these thirty-six, the *Lamed-Vov* as they are called. They are

> . . . indistinguishable from simple mortals; often they are unaware of their station. But if just one of them were lacking, the sufferings of mankind would poison even the souls of the newborn, and humanity would suffocate with a single cry. For the Lamed-Vov are the hearts of the world multiplied, and into them, as into one receptacle, pour all our griefs . . . The most pitiable are the Lamed-Vov who remain unknown to themselves. For those the spectacle of the world is an unspeakable hell. . . . "When an unknown Just rises to Heaven," a Hasidic story goes, "he is so frozen that God must warm him for a thousand years between His fingers before his soul can open itself to Paradise. And it is known that some remain forever inconsolable at human woe, so that God Himself cannot warm them. So from time to time the Creator, blessed be His name, sets forward the clock of the Last Judgment by one minute."[8]

Notes

1. Toni Morrison, in *Black Women Writers at Work*, edited by Claudia Tate, New York: Continuum, 1984, pp. 128–9.